Helping
Destitute Men

John Leach
and John Wing

Helping
Destitute Men

TAVISTOCK PUBLICATIONS

First published in 1980 by
Tavistock Publications Ltd
11 New Fetter Lane, London EC4P 4EE
Published in the USA *by*
Tavistock Publications
in association with Methuen, Inc.
733 *Third Avenue, New York,* NY 10017

© 1980 *J. Leach and J. K. Wing*

Photoset by Northampton Phototypesetters Ltd
and printed in Great Britain at the
University Press, Cambridge

ISBN 0 422 76760 3 *(hardback edition)*

British Library Cataloguing in Publication Data

Leach, John
Helping destitute men.
1. Relief stations (for the poor) – Great Britain
– Case studies
2. Camberwell Reception Centre
3. St Mungo Community Trust
I. Title   II. Wing, John Kenneth
362.8   HV4545.A4   80-40092
ISBN 0-422-76760-3

Contents

Preface

This book is concerned with the most severe forms of destitution, experienced by men who 'sleep rough' or use night shelters or reception centres for prolonged periods. Such destitution is a paradox in a welfare state and there have been many attempts to explain why it persists in spite of the efforts of humane reformers to prevent it. Many of these explanations are derived from some form of ideology – a set of beliefs concerning the nature of the good society – rather than from a testable theory. Others, equally difficult to test, are based on convictions about the moral or constitutional make-up of people who become destitute. Yet others, perhaps more plausible, assume that there are many paths towards destitution, and many combinations of causes, so that no simple means of prevention is likely to be effective. We review these theories briefly because they affect the attitudes and practices of those who try to help men who have already become destitute. The research described in the book was undertaken in order to evaluate the efforts made by two apparently very different types of service, one statutory, the other voluntary, in the hope that practical recommendations could be made concerning the forms of help that would be of immediate benefit. We were not principally concerned with primary prevention but with the rehabilitation and long-term settlement of severely disadvantaged and disabled people.

There is no substantial body of research to build upon. Previous studies have often been selective, narrow in orientation, crude in descriptive technique and uncritical in conclusions. This has been due to the fact that they were undertaken by practitioners – usually doctors or social workers – who were appalled by the conditions they observed and, without great pretence at methodological expertise, wanted to make a contribution towards their betterment. A literature of this kind can be found in the early stages of all attempts to specify the principles of good practice, whatever branch of the helping professions is involved. The problems of obtaining proper samples, designing studies that would allow some degree of hypothesis-testing, constructing instruments for systematic and comprehensive description of relevant behaviour and attitudes, and, above all, obtaining reliable information from men who might reasonably regard personal questions with suspicion, are probably more formidable than in any other area of social research. Earlier work has been severely criticized on these grounds but it should not be dismissed altogether; nor should it be concluded that nothing at all can be done to improve the choice between conflicting theories. Progress may be slow but there is no reason to suppose that real knowledge cannot be accumulated in this field as in any other.

We cannot claim to have solved the problems encountered by our predecessors. Indeed, we have deliberately kept our research procedures and analysis very simple compared with other studies undertaken by the MRC Social Psychiatry Unit, under whose auspices this research was carried out. We did not think our data could carry the weight either of a sophisticated statistical analysis or of a complex theoretical interpretation. We do consider, and must leave the reader to decide how far we are justified, that the long time period covered by the research, the fact that members of the research team were able to come very close to the problems they were studying, the action research design of part of the work, and the use of similar data-gathering techniques in two different types of service system, constitute an advance on earlier studies and can, in turn, provide a basis for better work in the future. Our tentative conclusions about the kinds of help most likely to be useful to men who have long been severely destitute are derived from work in both voluntary and statutory organizations and are, in many ways, similar to those of people with substantial practical experience of the health and social services. We hope they will receive serious attention and that the lives of at least some destitute men will become richer and more independent in consequence.

In any research of the kind we have carried out it is axiomatic that no theories could have been tested, no results obtained, no conclusions drawn, and no recommendations made without the help of the people principally concerned; in this case, men on the streets, in houses, shelters, and centres for the destitute.

We are indebted to the Trustees, Director, and Staff of the St Mungo Community Trust for their collaboration in this research and to the Department of Health for its support. The Managers and Staff of the Camberwell reception centre, its Battersea Annexe, and two smaller Centres, provided us with all the help we asked for.

In examining the effectiveness of any service, it is impossible not to appear to be examining the effectiveness of those who operate it. Evaluative work may seem, at certain points, a scrutiny of individuals rather than of structures or of events. At no time, however, did we feel under pressure to modify our approaches or ideas, either from the organizations we were investigating or from the Department of Health. We always welcomed the frank expression of views, and often received blasts from every side, but our opinions are our own responsibility.

During the pilot survey, in late 1971 and early 1972, Dr Justin Schlicht undertook the psychiatric examinations and Dr Harry Dawson was responsible for compiling histories and for obtaining follow-up information. Mrs Seta Waller processed the data and began the statistical register. Mrs Susan Pettigrew replaced Mrs Waller in November 1972, at first full-time and later part-time. She undertook the follow-up surveys. Miss Hazel Houghton helped with staff interviewing, during the latter part of 1972, by courtesy of DHSS. Miss Ruth Sousa and Miss Janice Nixon helped with the statistical analysis. Miss Joan Jenkins and Mrs Jackie Marshall acted as part-time clerical assistants. Miss Irene Barker helped substantially with the 'peripatetic survey'. Although this sounds like a large team, during nearly all the period of research the grant from DHSS supported one full-time sociologist and two part-time clerical assistants.

Mrs Hazel Gosling and Miss Christine Durston patiently typed innumerable drafts of this book.

All in all, we have been most fortunate in our collaborators and are duly grateful.

1 Concepts of destitution: Statutory and voluntary approaches

Introduction

We shall be concerned, in this book, with what we call severe and chronic destitution, that is, with the problems of people (nearly always men) who frequently sleep rough or use night shelters or reception centres over a long period of time. These men are, by definition, disadvantaged, homeless, and living outside a family setting. They are often, therefore, called 'homeless single persons'. However, this term also includes two much larger groups of people with whom we are only concerned insofar as they are at higher risk of joining the severely destitute. One of these groups consists of men who habitually use common lodging houses or large hostels. The other consists of people who have lived for a long time in institutions such as prisons or psychiatric hospitals, or are constantly moving in and out of such environments, and who have no other home or resources of their own. There are yet other overlapping groups, such as those with living-in jobs, particularly in the hotel trade, or who do casual unskilled work in the building industry, moving from site to site with frequent periods of unemployment.

Members of these overlapping groups do from time to time use reception centres and night shelters and, to this extent, become represented in our research, but we shall concentrate mainly on the problems of those who do so over long periods of time. Our main aim is to contribute to knowledge of how to help such men.

By defining the group in this empirical way we are not only selecting the most disadvantaged, and probably the neediest, men in our society but we are avoiding a definition in terms of some common set of personality characteristics or of vague attributions such as 'vagrant', 'alcoholic', etc. We shall investigate the possibility of classifying *problems* but that is not at all the same thing as classifying *persons*.

Since the difficulties experienced by destitute men* are likely to merge into broader and commoner problems such as long-term poverty due to low wages, chronic unemployment, housing shortages resulting in family homelessness or overcrowding, deprivation during childhood, group prejudice, and physical and mental disease and disability, we shall begin with a brief review of the way that social policy has developed in response to changing concepts of prevention and relief. We shall illustrate this review by a more detailed description of two particular organizations. The first is the Camberwell Reception Centre, administered by the Supplementary Benefits Commission for the purpose of accommodating men who have no means of support. The second is the St Mungo Community, a voluntary organization working with men 'on the streets' as well as providing various forms of residential accommodation. The services of these two agencies formed the subject of most of the research described in this book. A review of previous research into these and other services for the destitute will be found in Chapter 2.

The development of government policy

It is impossible to understand contemporary attitudes to destitution without some consideration of the principles underlying the 1834 Poor Law Amendment Act (the so-called New Poor Law) which were themselves derived from more general social, economic, and political attitudes widely held at that time. It was assumed that, with certain

---

*From now on the term 'destitute', unless specified otherwise, will be used to mean 'severely and chronically destitute'.

exceptions, riches were the reward for enterprise and hard work and that poverty was the result of fecklessness and sloth. Whatever was spent on the poor must come out of the pockets of the better off. Public relief would be likely to encourage idleness and to decrease the motivation of the honest working population. The remedy was to ensure that the most exacting, unpleasant and badly paid job would be pleasurable and rewarding by comparison with accepting relief. This was the principle of 'less eligibility'.

In accordance with this principle relief was made available only in workhouses where the conditions of life were rendered deliberately punitive. Families were split up, work was monotonous and back-breaking, there was no leisure time, food was poor and scanty, and the supervision often authoritarian and hostile. Some workhouses applied these rules with discrimination (Fraser 1976) but others pursued them with rigour, producing appalling conditions (Anstruther 1973).

Although the architects of the Poor Law had recommended separate independently-managed institutions for children, the ill, and the infirm (their main concern being able-bodied paupers), General Mixed Workhouses remained in general use. Casual wards (or 'spikes') were set up for vagrants. As late as the first decade of the twentieth century, two-thirds of the sick and infirm inmates of Poor Law Institutions (estimated to number at least 130,000) were placed in General Mixed Workhouses (Webb and Webb 1909). The grim conditions of these institutions ('a reproach and disgrace peculiar to England' (Webb and Webb 1929: 5)) and their lack of any remedial or rehabilitative element evoked widespread censure. The Webbs noted the conclusions of a foreign observer, made in 1871:

'The workhouse purports at one and the same time to be: (i) a place where able-bodied adults who cannot or will not find employment are set to work; (ii) an asylum for the aged, the blind, the deaf and dumb or otherwise incapacitated for labour; (iii) a hospital for the sick poor; (iv) a school for orphans, foundlings, and other poor children; (v) a lying-in home for poor mothers; (vi) an asylum for those of unsound mind not being actually dangerous; (vii) a restingplace for such vagabonds as it is not deemed possible or desirable to send to prison. The combination of such mutually inconsistent purposes renders the administration defective as regards each one of them . . .' (Webb and Webb 1929: 138).

4 Helping Destitute Men

Criticisms of this kind were part of a reaction, in the second half of the nineteenth century, against the harshness of poor law administration. There was increasing pressure for change, a process accelerated by the 1884 extension of the franchise (nearly tripling the county electorate) and the pioneering inquiries of investigators like Charles Booth, who showed that poverty was not necessarily synonymous with moral weakness, but could be caused by many other factors. The expansion of lodging house provision in the latter half of the nineteenth century was expressed, as Archard points out, 'in terms of a policy of "housing the homeless poor" who, due to economic forces, consisted mainly of individuals who were temporarily or permanently separated from their family households' (Archard 1973: 147).

In response to demands for change, a succession of minor reforms modified poor law administration during the 1890s. In 1894, for example, it became permissible for workhouse officials to distribute dry tea, milk, and sugar for women to make their own afternoon tea; in 1897 trained nurses were allowed to be employed for the care of the sick poor. A further consequence of the changing climate of opinion was the setting up, in 1905, of a Royal Commission on the Poor Laws. The recommendations of the commissioners, and the divergence between the Majority (sixteen) and Minority (four) groups, reflected changing attitudes to poverty and the role of government. Both groups advocated the provision of specialized facilities for different categories of poor people. Both felt that the General Mixed Workhouses served no useful purpose and should be abolished. However, while the Majority recommended a modified Poor Law system (based on new 'public assistance authorities') the Minority (led by Beatrice Webb) advocated a radical departure from the existing system. They felt that the Poor Law was intrinsically bad and recommended its abolition. In their view the State should aim to prevent rather than palliate destitution and, to this end, should provide specialized municipal services dealing separately with each category of non-able-bodied person. The 'cleavage in spirit' between the two groups reflected, the Webbs suggested, the difference between repression and 'a Framework of Prevention . . . which embraced, not "destitute" persons in respect of their destitution, but the whole population, in respect of their particular needs' (Webb and Webb 1929: 546).

It was not until the Poor Law Act of 1930, however, that the administration of poor relief was taken over by the local authorities. The Act was preceded by the enquiries of a Departmental Committee which investigated the characteristics of casual ward users. The differing needs of these individuals, and the inappropriateness of housing them in a single institution, resulted in recommendations for the referral of persons in certain categories to outside agencies, for example, voluntary organizations for retraining unemployed youths, hospitals for the sick, and institutions for the women. The setting up of hostels for men whose chances of resettlement appeared good was advised. There were no specific recommendations concerning the mentally ill, mentally handicapped, and alcoholic inmates (about a quarter of the total) (Tidmarsh and Wood 1972a).

With the outbreak of war in 1939, able-bodied destitute men were conscripted and many casual wards closed down. From an all-time high of 16,911 on 27 May 1932, the numbers in 'spikes' dropped to a few thousand (Stewart 1975). After the war, in its Circular 136/46 (Ministry of Health 1946), the Ministry of Health laid down a new policy designed to abolish the casual ward system and eradicate destitution.

The strategy of the Circular was to identify the needs of destitute sub-groups and meet them by referral to specialized services. Thus, given that such services could be provided, an accumulation of the homeless in modern equivalents of the old mixed workhouse would be avoided. Seven categories of men were described and a specific policy recommended in each case (Wood 1976).

(1) Those in work and lacking shelter were to be provided with temporary accommodation.
(2) Those desiring work were to be sent to the placing officer of the local employment exchange.
(3) The disabled were to be sent to the Disablement Rehabilitation Officer.
(4) Those disabled persons considered to be capable of work after medical treatment were to be sent to the appropriate agency.
(5) Young persons in need of 'mental or moral rehabilitation' were to be restored to their families or sent to a voluntary hostel.
(6) The 'hard core' of habitual vagrants were also to be given suitable treatment or when necessary dealt with by firmness to discourage 'vagabondage'.
(7) Those incapable of work and unsuitable for training were to be encouraged to enter an institution.

The authors of the Circular suggested that local authority 'case work' during the second world war had reduced the number of 'hard core' vagrants and that a similar policy would continue this process in the post-war period. A system of hostels was recommended to supplement the training and rehabilitative facilities provided by the Ministry of Labour and no doubts were expressed concerning the eventual achievement of resettlement. The post-war policy inaugurated by Circular 136/46 was part of a more comprehensive approach to social planning, reflecting the ideas put forward by Beatrice Webb and consolidating the rejection of the ideas of the New Poor Law. The assumption that government policies would ensure the continuation of the full employment maintained during the war led to the belief that much 'casual' destitution would be prevented. The system of Industrial Rehabilitation Units, Government Training Centres, and Remploy factories set up by the 1944 Disabled Persons Act, would help those who needed rehabilitation and retraining. The aged, sick, and handicapped would be looked after by the appropriate health and social services. This left a relatively small group of people who were destitute, it was believed, not only because of social disadvantage but because of personal 'inadequacy', who found it difficult 'to fit in with society and to cooperate with people helping them'.* Much emphasis was placed, in the Circular, on the remedial value of case-work with this group.

The National Assistance Act, which came into operation on 5 July 1948, put into effect the principles of Circular 136/46. 'The existing poor law under which relief of the poor was undertaken by local authorities was repealed and in its place there was established a system of national assistance administered by the National Assistance Board, and financed out of monies provided by Parliament' (Halsbury 1959: 454). The new Board was given the duty

'to assist all persons in Great Britain who are without resources to meet their requirements. . . . Furthermore, every local authority is under a duty to provide both residential accommodation for persons who, by reason of age, infirmity or any other circumstances, are in need of care and attention which is not otherwise available to them, and temporary accommodation for persons urgently in need of it owing to circumstances which they could not reasonably have

---

* This quotation is taken from a later document, *Homeless Single Persons* (see Chapter 2); but the problem of this 'hard core' was already evident in 1946.

foreseen or in such other circumstances as the local authority may determine in any particular case' (Halsbury 1959: 454).

The Board (or local authorities acting as its agents) had a duty to provide temporary board and lodging in 'reception centres' for 'people without a settled way of living'. The function of centres was, with the aid of case work, to effect the resettlement of clients. The criteria of resettlement were not specified, however, nor was there any consideration of whether those 'without a settled way of living' were a homogeneous group. The role of the reception centre with regard to the handicapped was not made explicit though it seems likely that the framers of the Act intended that handicapped people should be looked after by local authority services, leaving reception centres for the able-bodied. The difficulty of making this distinction was referred to in the 1976 Annual Report of the Supplementary Benefits Commission (SBC 1977) which pointed out that even at the time it was acknowledged

'that many of those using casual wards and workhouses were not "tramps" in the accepted sense, nor were they all capable of fending for themselves without some support. The principal need of some was for institutional care and attention (which made them still the responsibility of the local authority), while others needed only permanent accommodation, which the NAB was not empowered to provide.'

A related issue, hotly debated in 1948, concerned the concentration of destitute people in certain districts. 'It was regarded as unfair to local ratepayers that the cost of dealing with a shifting population should fall heaviest where the largest number happened to go . . .' (SBC 1977). These problems, still unresolved, will be considered again in Chapter 7.

According to the National Assistance Act, men were to be admitted to reception centres if staff thought they were leading an 'unsettled way of life' characterized by the frequent use of lodging houses and of periods spent sleeping rough.* 'Unless otherwise directed a new arrival . . . must be bathed and his clothing may be surrendered for drying and disinfection. He must, if required, submit himself for

---

*Exceptions to this occur when men are temporarily without resources, have no alternative source of accommodation and require 'tiding-over'.

medical examination and do such works as he may be required to do in assisting the running of the centre.' On the morning after their arrival men were to be interviewed and, on the completion of 'task work', were free to leave. Referrals to hospitals would be made where appropriate. Some men, who stayed more than one night, would be taken into 'residence' and receive a personal allowance. Those who found work would be charged for their board and lodging but were not required to leave the centre if in employment. Eventually it was intended that such men should be helped to find 'suitable' accommodation and so become resettled. 'Suitable' accommodation, for many NAB officers, seems to have meant 'an accommodating landlady' (Stewart 1975: 60).

Since the National Assistance Board had no new premises, reception centres were situated next to hospitals and local authority Part III accommodation. This resulted in pressure from hospital management committees and local authorities to close the centres down, the presence of casuals being considered unacceptable to patients and those in 'settled' residential care. The Board, in its turn, found that many centres were under-used and followed a policy of shutting them where possible. Of the 270 institutions taken over by the Board and utilized as reception centres, 136 were promptly closed. By 1970 the number of centres had declined to seventeen.

The Camberwell Reception Centre

By far the largest was the Camberwell Reception Centre which was built in 1878 as a Poor Law Institution (Tidmarsh and Wood 1972a). The premises were used during the Second World War for families made homeless through bombing and for refugees. In 1944 the buildings were opened as casual wards and in July 1948, under the National Assistance Act, they became a reception centre administered by the London County Council. As a consequence of local government reorganization the National Assistance Board assumed direct administration in February 1965.

The centre is situated on a site of about two and a half acres. The buildings have three stories and are grim and forbidding in appearance. Accommodation is in large open dormitories, with separate wings for users who stay only one night and for longer-term residents. There is a single large dining hall. Radical improvements to the existing premises would have necessitated enormous expenditure, and as it was early declared policy to tackle the problem of the size of the centre by dispersing residents to a network of smaller centres throughout London, only essential maintenance has been undertaken. The centre has 755 beds but provision can be made for many more. During the post-war years the number of residents on any given night has averaged about 500, though there was a gradual increase after 1954, reaching an average of more than 800 in 1972, when some 8,000 men passed through the Centre. Since then the numbers have declined again and are now between four and five hundred. The numbers are always much higher in the winter months.

The Reception Centre provides each man with a supper and bed for the night. In return, he has to agree to have a bath and to disinfestation when necessary. No alcohol or drugs are allowed on the premises. Rules of orderly behaviour have to be observed or the man will be evicted. There is a welfare section where some of the men are interviewed and assessed in order, when possible, to offer help which might encourage them to lead a more settled life. This help can range from social agencies to landladies. The Department of Employment maintains an office on the site in order to help men obtain employment or register for benefit. There is a 15-bed sick bay and a 12-bed dormitory for claimants who need minor treatments or bed rest.

More than half the men attending at any one time are 'residents' who have agreed to stay for some time. They have separate quarters. Some of these men work outside the Centre; others work inside, cleaning, preparing food, or working in the workshops. The rest of the men are 'casuals', attending on a daily basis.

The routines of the centre are supervised by Assistants. No special experience or qualifications are necessary to be an Assistant and vacancies have been filled by local recruitment. Salaries were linked with analogous local authority grades (e.g. Part III Care Assistants) but in April 1975 they became assimilated into the general service grades of the Civil Service, with pay and conditions of service linked to those of the messenger grade.

Detailed surveys conducted at the Centre between 1970 and 1972 will be considered in Chapter 2. The smaller centres designed to replace Camberwell in due course are described in Chapter 6.

Difficulties in carrying out NAB policy

It was apparent very early on that there would be difficulty in carrying out the policy first set out in Circular 136/46. At Camberwell, for example, 'by October 1947, none of the men referred to the Disablement Resettlement Officer had been accepted for training, some 140 old men had accumulated and the numbers in the institution had risen from 182 in September 1946 to 392 in September 1947' (Tidmarsh and Wood 1972a). The problem of 'the accumulation of the long-stay' had already begun. Great difficulties were encountered in resettling or transferring the disabled, particularly the mentally ill and retarded. An early emphasis on firm administration (e.g. prosecuting users for deliberate self-neglect) had little effect. Few men were placed into jobs. Within a year of the inauguration of the NAB employers in some areas were so disheartened by the poor performance of people referred from reception centres that they became reluctant to take on any more. Stewart has commented that 'the early NAB reports can be seen as catalogues of despair' (Stewart 1975: 147).

However, as we have seen, the principles underlying the NAB policy were thought to be right, and it was assumed that the gradual establishment of a wide network of social and medical services, together with full employment, universal education, and proper pensions and benefits, would eventually be effective. The prevailing view was one of complacency. Brandon, whose work was to be influential in focusing attention on the problems of homeless single people, has described the climate of opinion in the 1950s and early 1960s. Single homelessness '. . . seemed to be a growing problem about which very little was known and in which hardly anyone was interested. Newspapers would not print stories about it; radio programmes would not broadcast about it and social workers ignored homelessness and busied themselves with their case conferences' (Brandon 1974: 16). To his reports on conditions in lodging houses and the numbers sleeping rough '. . . the local government ripostes were, 'it used to be very much worse until recently' or, 'we are going to hand it over to another authority very shortly. No sense in doing much'. Interest was at a very low level and change took place very slowly indeed' (Brandon 1974: 16).

But then, with an air of rediscovery (resembling, in many respects, Cohen's condition of 'moral panic' (Cohen 1972)) destitution quite suddenly became news. The subject was taken up by a new 'voluntary social work movement' concerned with a broad range of social problems and influenced by far-reaching theories about their origin and maintenance. This new movement attracted considerable publicity and its activities were an important factor in the Government's decision, in 1964–5, to 'obtain factual information which would enable the interested Government Departments and voluntary bodies to gauge better the size, nature and location [of the problems] of homelessness, vagrancy and social inadequacy' (NAB 1966). The National Assistance Board, which had been due to carry out an investigation of reception centres at the end of 1965, planned a more ambitious survey (including persons sleeping rough and living in common lodging houses, hostels, and shelters) because in 1964 and 1965, 'a number of voluntary bodies expressed concern both to the Government and to Government Departments about what they regarded as the increasing problem of the misfits and drifters of society, particularly those who habitually live in lodging-houses and hostels or sleep rough. This concern was not in itself by any means new, but it was clear that the problem was attracting increased public attention . . .' (NAB 1966: 1).*

There were, in fact, three main reasons why the NAB's policies were not proving successful. One was that some unemployment had persisted, so that the 'pool' of men who needed to make occasional use of services for the destitute had not greatly diminished. The second was that the supply of cheap accommodation for single men with low incomes was declining. The third was that community services for handicapped people were not being set up on an adequate scale, while a new trend towards emptying mental hospitals resulted in much larger numbers in need of such services.

The decline in lodging house and cheap hostel accommodation occurred at the same time as the decrease in places available in reception centres. The immediate reason for the decline was the redevelopment of central city areas and a recognition that the sites of cheap commercial hotels were of considerable value and could be put to more profitable use. Brandon, in an article prompted by the closure in 1972 of Butterwick House† in Hammersmith, with the loss of 750 beds, estimated that the number of lodging house beds in London, Manchester and Birmingham had almost halved between 1960 and 1972 (Brandon 1972). Butterwick House was demolished to make

---

* At the time of finalizing this work, in January 1979, there is another wave of public concern due to allegations of neglect and ill-treatment.
† One of the hotels operated by Rowton Houses Ltd.

way for a hotel and offices as part of the Borough's redevelopment plan although, at that time, there were alternative places available for only one-fifth of the men made homeless by its closure.

Wood, considering the implications of changes in the post-war housing situation for the residents of Camberwell Reception Centre, noted the 'gross shortage of accommodation' available to them (Wood 1976). She thought that the decline in rented and lodging house accommodation was particularly significant. In 1950, 45 per cent of all dwellings in the UK were rented from private owners; in 1973, only 17 per cent. The decline in amount of cheap accommodation available in hostels and lodging houses is best illustrated by figures from the survey carried out in 1972 by the Office of Population Censuses and Surveys (Digby 1976), compared with the position found in the earlier survey carried out by the NAB in 1965 (NAB 1966). There was a decrease from 37,845 to 31,253 beds. In fact more than half of the 1965 establishments, mostly smaller ones operated commercially, had closed, but there was some replacement by small voluntary hostels and shelters. There were 26,823 people in the 1972 census – an occupancy of 86 per cent. About 2,000 people use reception centres on any given night with about a further 1,000 in voluntary shelters which are subsidized by the Supplementary Benefits Commission.

The decline of the large mental hospital

Kathleen Jones has traced the evolution of public mental hospitals, from their origin as small asylums set up in reaction against the cruel or neglectful way in which the mentally disordered were dealt with in workhouses and in private care, through the long custodial era (from the 1870s to the 1940s) to the subsequent period of renewed therapeutic activity during the 1950s as a result of which the numbers of patients began to fall (Jones 1972). This long history does not allow for any simple explanation but the theories put forward at various times to account for mental disorder and to suggest how it should be treated parallel very closely certain aspects of the development of theories about destitution. David Rothman (Rothman 1971) has suggested that many types of institution (workhouses, hospitals, prisons, orphanages, etc.) passed through similar evolutionary phases. Early nineteenth century theories of training and segregation, according to Rothman, were initially based on the idea that much social deviance had its origin in the ideas of freedom fostered by the Enlightenment. Corrective training was required in order to instil good habits of work and life and the right attitudes to society. The institutions in which these ideas were put into practice lasted long after 'moral treatment' had been abandoned.

The influx of a new generation of psychiatrists after the Second World War, influenced by the ideas of social reform then in the air, and the establishment of a National Health Service integrating the mental hospitals and ex-workhouse infirmaries into a single system with the voluntary hospitals, led to a new spirit of optimism. Earlier ideas of moral treatment were revived and extended: open doors, the therapeutic community (a group psychoanalytic technique which turned into an anti-authoritarian movement), rehabilitation through the provision of meaningful domestic, social, and occupational roles, early resettlement outside hospital through the use of day centres, half-way houses, hostels, and sheltered work. It was recognized both that 'institutionalism' could be harmful and that it could often be overcome (Wing and Brown 1970).

Such efforts were successful, to a large extent, in replacing custodial attitudes by therapeutic ones in the pioneering hospitals, where the numbers of occupied beds began to decline well before the introduction of the phenothiazine drugs. The new forms of medication made it possible for other hospitals to follow the lead of the pioneers. In 1955 the national figures for England and Wales showed a decrease in occupied beds and there has been a steady decline since. This extension of the trend to hospitals where social treatments had not been fully developed was not an unmixed blessing. As in the case of Rothman's institutions which were regarded as beneficient *in them-selves* long after their educational regimes had deteriorated into mere custodialism, so discharge from hospital sometimes came to be regarded, *in itself*, as evidence of improvement and even cure.

The Mental Health Act of 1959 gave legislative sanction to the practice already adopted in the best hospitals, where 'desegregated' units had been introduced so that patients could be admitted without formality, and made it possible for compulsory admission for treatment to take place without the intervention of a magistrate. The 1962 national plan for England and Wales looked forward to a time when small psychiatric units attached to district general hospitals would be able to cope with most acute psychiatric illness while the social functions of the large hospitals would be taken over by the social service departments of local authorities.

It was noticed, however, that a large number of patients of 'no fixed abode' were being admitted to some mental hospitals. These men, moving around a circuit of lodging houses, reception centres, police cells, and sleeping rough, had little prospect of rehabilitation in hospital. In any case, many did not wish to stay. Whiteley, commenting on the prospects of the homeless ex-psychiatric patient, noted that 'at the time when the recovering psychiatric invalid needs the security of his family and home and the assurance and encouragement of his friends and relatives, the homeless man is returned to the cold solitude of his bunk in a friendless dormitory. There is little hope of rehabilitation – the climb is too severe – and he relapses and continues to relapse, and the accumulation of similar cases continues' (Whiteley 1958). Berry and Orwin (1966) found that the admission rate of patients of 'no fixed abode' to a Birmingham mental hospital in 1964 was three times higher than in 1959. Rollin (1963) noted a five-fold increase of such patients to Horton hospital between 1959 and 1961.

In addition to this particular problem there was a more general one. The alternative services that were supposed to be made available outside hospital were not in fact set up in sufficient numbers. The emphasis was on 'half-way houses', intended to have a rehabilitative function like the hospitals themselves. Residents were expected to move to more independent accommodation after a fixed period of time, usually a year or less, but it was found that many were too disabled to be resettled in this way and therefore accumulated as a long-stay group. Fears were expressed that hostels, far from being rehabilitative, would simply become 'back wards' in the community (Apte 1968).

More recent studies have not confirmed these particular fears but they have suggested that the goal of resettlement through rehabilitation is often illusory and that many patients discharged from mental hospitals require long-term care and shelter rather than treatment (Wing and Olsen 1979). Long-term groups are also accumulating in day centres (Wing and Hailey 1972) and in psychiatric hospitals – the latter much smaller than in the past but presenting difficult problems because of the nature of their disabilities (Mann and Cree 1976). Finally, recent research has emphasized the problems of relatives, who are the main supporters of many severely disabled people 'in the community' and are often not receiving the help and support they need (Creer and Wing 1974). It is not surprising that some patients move away from their families and are at risk of becoming destitute. This risk is present even in an area with relatively good services. The most recent government statement has acknowledged the problems, but it is not yet clear how they will be met (DHSS 1975).

This brief review of developments in the mental health services is relevant to the problem of destitution in two ways. In the first place, many chronically destitute people have been in mental hospitals and received psychiatric diagnoses (see Chapter 2 for a review of surveys demonstrating this). In the second place, many of the new theoretical approaches to destitution have been influenced by, and occasionally derived from, new theories about the genesis and maintenance of mental illnesses, particularly schizophrenia, which have been subsumed under the more general heading of 'social deviance'.

Part, at least, of the reaction against the large old-fashioned mental hospitals was due to a rejection of the assumption that the condition of long-stay patients with a diagnosis of 'schizophrenia' (more than half of the chronic population) was entirely due to an inevitable deterioration supposed to be characteristic of that disease. A moderate statement of the new position is that many people admitted to hospital in the old days were socially disadvantaged. They had few roots in a local community, exiguous links with their families, poor social skills, and no great motivation to leave hospital once established as inmates. Once the acute phase of the disorder was over (before the introduction of the new medications this could have been several years) the expectation was that they would remain in hospital indefinitely. The longer they did so the less determined were they to leave. There were three elements, therefore, in the chronic state: illness and subsequent disability (which could vary from mild to severe and from stable to unstable), prior social disadvantage, and 'institutionalism' (a secondarily acquired disinclination to resume everyday life outside hospital) (Wing and Brown 1970).

This formulation does not assume that no disability is present but accepts that disability can be maintained and increased in the socially poverty-stricken environments of poor hospitals, particularly those approximating to what Erving Goffman called 'total institutions' (1961). Similar principles can be applied to other residential and day environments: social disablement is always due to a mixture of handicapping factors – intrinsic impairment, social disadvantage, and secondary reaction (Wing and Olsen 1979). Much of the early success of techniques of rehabilitation, according to this view, lay in undoing the harm that had been caused by poor environments and prior disadvantage, by resocialization and retraining, and by ensuring, through attention to after-care, that extra disabilities did not accumulate on top of any that were 'intrinsic'. If proper attention were paid to these factors from the time of the first acute episode, the adventitious elements in chronic disability would be corrected or prevented, and any remaining symptoms or handicaps would require the provision of an appropriate degree of care and shelter.

A much more radical formulation denies any element due to disease or 'intrinsic' impairment. In the theories elaborated by Goffman (1959) and by Scheff (1966), the conditions diagnosed by psychiatrists as 'mental illness' (at least, those without an obvious organic pathology) are simply aspects of social deviance which happen to be controlled through the use of psychiatric terminology and 'treatment', in the interests of the present structure of power in society. The appropriate methods of prevention are therefore social and a variety of solutions have been proposed depending largely on the wider social and political theories of the proponents. These arguments have been discussed in detail elsewhere (Wing 1978) and will be considered in relation to destitution in the next section.

New approaches to the problem of destitution

Public concern with the problem of destitution in the mid 1960s was largely due to the efforts of newly founded voluntary organizations attempting to help people who were sleeping rough. These organizations were motivated in a variety of ways apart from their charitable desire to relieve the very obvious problems of men and women living in chronic poverty. The Simon Community, for example, was founded in 1963 by Anton Wallich-Clifford (1968, 1974) because his experience as a probation officer had convinced him that the statutory services were inadequate to cope with the problem of destitution. The original purpose of the Simon Community was described as one of developing an experimental venture in care with the aim of drawing public attention

'to an unrecognised and growing problem of people for whom there was no help, or who other organizations had left off caring for, because of their constant failure with these "hopeless cases". The

Simon Communities founded in different parts of the country lived at a level acceptable to the residents. They were decidedly anti-posh and somewhat inefficient. The Simonlight project for methylated spirit drinkers in London's East End used a condemned derelict house for its first tier care. Workers in Simon were not supposed to be "staff" but, as the "caring", they worked with the "cared-for" and lived with them as equally as possible. As a Community, Workers and Members shared food and accommodation. The Worker-Simons drew some £2 a week pay, roughly equivalent to what was drawn in cash by the Members from the Ministry of Social Security. The Community Members were themselves volunteers, co-operating with the Worker-Simons in self-help for themselves and for the neediest among them. The Simon Community accepted people as they were and not as they should have been. As a result of Simon care some Members were able to progress via other organizations to a point where they were able to find a place for themselves in society. Others used their progress to devote themselves as Workers-Simons alongside the outside recruited volunteers' (Tully 1970).

The Simon Community explicitly rejected materialism and showed a 'willingness to see Christ in even the most abandoned character' (Wallich-Clifford 1973: 164). Some supporters went further, and equated destitution with other-worldliness, seeing the life-style of destitute people as a manifestation of fundamental Christian values.

'Talking to down-and-outs is nearly always moving. In so many ways they follow the Christian tenets on which our society is supposed to be based better than us, the "successful" ones. They really do take no thought for the morrow. They don't seek to lay up worldly goods, they are truly meek and indeed again and again turn the other cheek to a society which seems almost to enjoy hitting them' (Sandford 1971: 34).

Even among those who were not motivated by religious values there was often a degree of admiration for people who had evidently so thoroughly rejected the style of life desired by most of their contemporaries – an admiration perhaps based on the assumption that the rejection had been made on intellectual grounds rather than out of necessity. 'Destitution' was regarded as a positive choice. However, most of the voluntary organizations adopted some form of the 'inadequacy' theory. Wallich-Clifford, for example, defined social inadequacy as 'the inability to face up to demands, responsibilities and pressures of life within the normal framework of society' (Wallich-Clifford 1973: 163). He added that the condition was recognized as a disease entity in Scandinavia and recommended that legislation in Britain should reflect this view. Matthews, similarly, spoke of 'two clear symptoms' of social inadequacy; 'an inability to maintain an adequate work pattern, and an inability to form emotionally satisfying relationships' (Matthews 1968: 356). He regarded the condition as the 'common denominator' of those the Simon Community worked with – 'dossers, alcoholics, drug addicts, the mentally disturbed, and so on' (Matthews 1968: 356).

This diversity of views, compatible with a wide range of theories of action, had as a unifying factor the assumption that the destitute were 'victims of society' who could only be helped within a setting where conventional social values were not accepted. The term 'community' was often used to describe the kind of environment the volunteers were attempting to create, the concept being derived in part from the idea of the 'therapeutic community' developed by psychiatrists fifteen years earlier. The major elements taken over were the blurring of authority boundaries and the sharing by all members (whether 'staff' or 'residents') of their daily experiences, relationships, and decisions. The communities were small and, ideally, approximated to the 'primary groups' described by Shils as possessing 'a high degree of solidarity, informality in the code of rules which regulate the behaviour of its members, and autonomy in the creation of these rules' (Shils 1951: 44). 'Doing your own thing' was the pervasive ethic and the development of each individual's potential the ultimate aim (Kanter 1972).

The volunteers believed that 'permissive' environments of this kind would facilitate an ability to form personal relationships in people who had previously been completely isolated and had spurned all efforts to get close to them. In Simon Community hostels, for example, 'someone will always be ready to listen, and any process of healing, of making a man whole again, takes place within a human relationship. Simon's work is conducted at an informal, even disorderly, level appropriate to the men we are working with – time spent trying to impose our own standards on the men would be time wasted' (Matthews 1968: 358). Within the hostels, Simon volunteers emphasized the need to 'identify' with residents by living alongside them twenty-four hours a day, sharing the same living conditions and making do with the same income.

There was, therefore, a certain unity in the views of the new voluntary movement but much of this was negative, being based on a rejection of 'the medical model' and the 'Poor Law' attitudes identified with the statutory services. Concepts of mental illness and disability were discounted, even as partial explanations of destitution. Destitute people were seen as 'inadequate', or unfortunate, or as harbingers of a new and better society. Whatever the explanation adopted, it was thought that the apparatus of the welfare state had failed. Reception centres, still often housed in former workhouse buildings (of which Camberwell was pre-eminently the symbol), were seen as an inadequate – not to say harmful – form of provision. Few of the young volunteers were enthusiastic about their contemporary society and much of their motivation for setting up the new communities stemmed from a conviction that there must be a better way to live.

The accommodation set up by the Simon Community was provided in hostels and shelters situated in inner-urban districts inhabited by destitute people. Young volunteer 'workers' lived under the same conditions as 'members', who were recruited from a soup run, or the streets. Different philosophies began to develop within different Simon groups, some radical, others more traditional, and a good deal of argument occurred between volunteers who had adopted opposing points of view.

Many newly developing organizations have discovered that the qualities necessary during a pioneering phase are not necessarily those needed for maintenance and further development. Frustrations occur and some Simon volunteers came to feel that the movement had lost its original drive and that new and more vigorous initiatives were required. Wallich-Clifford, himself, concluded in 1966 that '. . . something was missing. . . . The old spirit of campaigning had died on us' (Wallich-Clifford 1974: 136). A policy of financial retrenchment, initiated by the leadership, resulted in cutbacks in the Community's services and encouraged tendencies towards decentralization and schism. The centre of Simon's work had always been the East End of London. In 1969, however, '. . . with the growing Community undergoing radical and far-reaching structural changes, and with workers recruited and trained – or untrained, depending on finances – on a very different basis to our original close-knit and primarily-related little group, we withdrew from Bethnal Green' (Wallich-Clifford 1974: 139). The powerhouse of Simon ideals was divided as disillusioned volunteers went their separate ways but the schisms served to provide the motivation for other enterprises. The energies of the disillusioned were harnessed to new initiatives whose aim was to embody the ideals which had formed the first impetus of Simon. One such venture was called the St Mungo Community. The Simon organization continued in being, however, and now has communities in many parts of the country (Beswick 1978).

The origins and growth of the St Mungo Community 1969-71

In May 1969, the Simon Community decided to discontinue its London soup run as part of a policy of retrenchment. The soup run organizer decided to found a new organization, the St Mungo Community, with the aim of continuing the soup run's work. At that time, there were four worker members living in a small terraced house in Battersea, let to them by Wandsworth Council at a nominal rent. In May 1970, a second house was acquired from the Council, twelve doors down the road from the first. A month later, the Council gave St Mungo's a third house and, shortly afterwards, a fourth. Part of this fourth house was already occupied and it was used for offices.

The Director and the young volunteer staff who joined him regarded the soup run as important for two reasons. First, the soup and bread was believed to constitute the main meal of the day for many of the men contacted on the soup run. Second, the soup run was seen by the staff as a means of unpressurized contact with these men. The staff believed that destitute men were 'isolated', 'reticent', and 'suspicious'. In their view, such men would reject and avoid 'institutional' accommodation like government reception centres and common lodging houses. The staff emphasized, therefore, that destitute men should be initially met on their own 'territory' (the streets) and that they should be talked to as 'equals', i.e. with no attempt to establish a client-social worker relationship.

The St Mungo soup run operated every night of the year at six locations in the West End of London. This continuity was held to be vital by the staff. A document discussing the first year's work of the organization commented that the soup run was

'a means of communication which is designed to go out to meet people each and every night. . . . Its main function is to be there as a lifeline for people when and if they want to use it, as a means of extricating themselves from their present surroundings to people that they at least know. Continuity was and is an important factor. The fact that we are there night after night . . . We set up to show that we do care.'

The St Mungo volunteer staff were termed 'workers'. They were usually young people, in their late teens or early twenties, who, virtually unpaid, manned the St Mungo services. Of both sexes, and idealistic, the workers' aim was to create an informal, egalitarian 'community', which they would share with those destitute men who accepted this ideal. The workers hoped that giving out soup regularly and unconditionally would encourage some destitute men to develop close relationships with them. As a St Mungo pamphlet put it: 'by treating the people that we meet on the streets as equals, developing relationships and friendships, and showing that we do care, we are able to exercise our true intentions of companionship, compassion and practical help'.

The workers believed that they could help destitute men only if the latter 'related' to them. For this to occur sustained contact was necessary. Relationships initiated on the soup run were therefore developed in St Mungo hostels. The latter were short-lease terraced houses, capable of taking ten to fifteen 'residents' (the term given by St Mungo staff to men living in the houses) and two or three workers. Each house was leased from the local council at a nominal rent. There was a communal dining room in each house and, sometimes, a separate communal leisure room, where the men watched television and played games such as cards or draughts. Most residents shared a bedroom with one or two other residents. The number of single bedrooms varied but some bedrooms in all the houses were shared. They had wardrobes or cupboards for residents' belongings and the residents were free to decorate their section of the room with posters, paint, and personal belongings. Residents were not given their own house key. The weekly rent was about £5 per week in 1972. In the case of the unemployed, rent was deducted from their social security benefit. The workers were paid 'pocket money', the equivalent of an unemployed resident's benefit after rent had been deducted.

The workers enforced a 'no drink' rule to help men attempting to overcome alcoholism but otherwise the houses had few restrictions. For example, residents were free to help with cooking and housework or not, as they wished. An emphasis on informality was the keynote of the 'treatment'. In a 1971 document submitted to DHSS the St Mungo management described aspects of the house regime. 'Within his hostel,' they claimed, 'the resident finds himself quite free. . . . He may come and go as he pleases, even if he wishes to stay in bed all day.' The objective of this approach, the management said, was to demonstrate to residents that the word 'Community' had meaning.

'We call ourselves a community because our workers and our residents live together, sharing rooms, eating together and being financially on virtually the same level. In fact our residents who are not working receive from the state 3/- per week more than the staff receive in pocket money. Within this framework of near equality a resident very soon feels himself incorporated into a society, whereas before his arrival when he was still a vagrant he felt himself outside of any society.'

A regime of this kind, the management suggested, with its emphasis on equality and mutual respect, would result in residents developing a sense of their worth as individuals. This increased self-esteem, and the confidence that resulted from it, would form the basis of an eventual settlement in independent accommodation such as a flat or 'digs'. The process by which this would occur was not specified in any detail. All these ideas were clearly derived from Simon.

On 1 September 1970, St Mungo's received a grant from the Home Office 'to meet the deficit in the running costs of two houses parts of which we were using to house our ex-offenders' (of no fixed abode). At this time also a small expansion in staff numbers was taking place. By September 1970 the St Mungo Community had six full-time staff living in the houses and one person living out, who organized the soup run. The organization's financial position, however, even with the aid of a grant, was far from secure. 'We were still living from hand to mouth, relying totally on the public to support us financially and the Home Office grant to keep us out of the "red". . . . The financial policy of that time was to do first and think about the cost afterwards, it was what we had to do if we were to help these people.'

In January 1971, the St Mungo staff acquired their first house in the Notting Hill area from Westminster City Council and in the February of that year, the Council also leased them the adjoining house. The staff made the basement of the latter into a bigger soup kitchen. By March 1971, apart from volunteers who helped on the soup run one night a week, there were eleven full-time workers living in the houses and four people working in the St Mungo administrative offices.

In September 1971 the management applied for government funding and a grant was received from the Department of Health and Social Security supporting the work of the St Mungo Community on an experimental basis for a period of several years. One of the conditions of funding was that the grant should provide for a small research team in order to evaluate the effectiveness of the St Mungo services. The results of that research are described in Chapters 3 to 6.

Summary

Public policy towards the destitute since the Second World War, as expressed in official circulars and publications, has been motivated by a desire to abolish the remnants of Poor Law attitudes and practice and to substitute more humane principles of prevention and care. It was thought initially that full employment, universal education, and a national system of pensions and welfare benefits would lead fairly rapidly to the disappearance of serious poverty, while handicapped people would be cared for by a new network of health and social services. By the early 1960s, however, it was clear to many critics that these predictions were not being fulfilled. Unemployment had persisted, the supply of cheap accommodation available to single men on low incomes was declining, and the social welfare system did not prove adequate to the task of sustaining an adequate minimum standard of living for numerous disadvantaged groups.

This was particularly evident in the case of mentally disabled people discharged from large psychiatric hospitals, for whom inadequate alternative provision was made, in part, at least, because their disabilities were invisible and hence unrecognized. Destitute men continued to use reception centres and night shelters. The conditions of life there, though preferable to sleeping rough, were often squalid. The excellent intention to move away from Poor Law principles was vitiated by the fact that the buildings in which they were embodied continued to do duty as hospitals, welfare institutions, reception centres, and prisons. The message conveyed by these buildings was different from that of official statements and it was difficult to claim that the spirit of the Poor Law was dead while its fabric remained so evidently alive.

A new voluntary social work movement developed which pointed to the deficiencies in the statutory services and put forward a range of alternative solutions. These varied from simple gap-filling to radical proposals for preventing poverty by structural changes in society. Most of the new bodies put forward some form of inadequacy theory to account for the fact that only some disadvantaged and disabled people became destitute and there was considerable overlap between the ideas of those in the statutory and voluntary services. Nevertheless, it was difficult for the public service to rid itself of the Poor Law image while destitute men were sleeping in cardboard boxes on the Embankment, with the Camberwell Reception Centre as the main alternative offered in London by the NAB. The young volunteer workers who ran the soup run and houses set up by organizations such as the Simon Community were motivated by the ferment of religious, political, and social ideas in the air at that time. Their enthusiasm and dedication was attractive and they received a good deal of public sympathy.

In the next chapter, we shall discuss in more detail the reasons why the welfare policies of the immediate post-war years did not succeed in preventing destitution and consider the results of surveys of destitute people carried out during the past twenty-five years.

2 Social policies and social surveys

The broad framework of social policy

It is apparent from the discussion in Chapter 1 that destitution cannot be considered as an isolated phenomenon. Beatrice Webb and her colleagues were convinced that poverty bred further poverty and that a broad range of social services was needed in order to reduce disadvantage to a minimum. There is little doubt that much destitution was, in fact, prevented by the measures taken during and after the war. Even at its post-war peak, the number of men using the Camberwell Reception Centre (8,000 in 1972) never approached the pre-war maximum (17,000). It seems a reasonable assumption that further reduction is possible if detailed attention were paid to a wide variety of preventive measures. The kinds of action required can be illustrated by considering the broad aims of social policy as they have developed since the war. The policy had two main aims: first to establish a universal system of social security, second to ensure equal access to adequate education, medical treatment, welfare services, and housing.

The social insurance scheme was described in detail in the 1942 report of the Inter-Departmental Committee on 'Social Insurance and Allied Services' – the Beveridge Report. The Committee commented that

> 'under the scheme of social insurance, which forms the main feature of this plan, every citizen of working age will contribute in his appropriate class according to the security that he needs, or as a married woman will have contributions made by the husband. Each will be covered for all his needs by a single weekly contribution on one insurance document. All the principal cash payments – for unemployment, disability and retirement – will continue so long as the need lasts, without means test, and will be paid from a Social Insurance Fund built up by contributions from the insured persons, from their employers, if any, and from the State' (p. 11).

Cases of need not covered by insurance would be met by a system of national assistance. A 'real, if limited, continuing scope' (p. 141) for additional assistance was anticipated in certain classes of claimant – those failing to fulfil contribution conditions, those failing to fulfil conditions for benefit, those with 'abnormal needs in respect of diet, care and other matters' (p. 142), and those in need through causes not suitable for insurance, e.g. some forms of desertion or separation. In general, however, national assistance was regarded as a minor and diminishing part of the work of the Ministry of Social Security. Given the adoption of the social insurance plan, and the maintenance of post-war employment, the committee believed that 'freedom from want should be regarded as a post-war aim capable of early attainment' (p. 168).

This view proved over-optimistic, however, and neither of the aims of the social welfare services was completely achieved. The insurance system did not reduce the numbers requiring additional benefits because the income deriving from a flat rate insurance scheme was not adequate to catch up with the post-war rise in the cost of living. Nor were changes in health and education provision completely successful in reducing inequality of opportunity. One consequence of these failures was the persistence of poverty.

Townsend's 1957 study, *The Family Life of Old People*, showed that three out of four of the retired people in the sample had an income low enough to qualify for national assistance (Townsend 1957). Nor was poverty confined to the elderly. Addressing the 1962 Conference of the British Sociological Association, Townsend (discussing data from the 1953-4 Family Expenditure Survey) pointed out that a third of households living at a standard less than 40 per cent above the basic national assistance rate had a head employed in full-time work. This finding was confirmed by the data presented in *The Poor and the Poorest* (Abel-Smith and Townsend 1965), a study which, in the authors' view, showed the minimal extent of poverty rather than its full dimensions. Atkinson, discussing the available evidence on low income in Britain, concluded that

'a significant minority of the population (between 4% and 9%) have incomes which are below the poverty line adopted in this study – the 'natural minimum' defined by the government through the Supplementary Benefit scale. A large proportion of these people are receiving pensions or other social security benefits, but a considerable number are people living in households which fall below the poverty line even though supported by a man in full-time work' (Atkinson 1969: 96).

A recent report on low pay in the hotel and catering trade (Brown and Winyard 1975) gives information about an industry which is notorious for its pockets of poverty and which has special relevance to our own enquiries, since many destitute men have previously worked as kitchen hands or porters. In 1974, the 'low pay cut-off' was £30 for a forty-hour week, but 30 per cent of full-time kitchen porters were receiving less than £20. (Very few received any income from tips.) Nearly half were in casual work, which meant only two to three days' work a week, averaging £3.80 a day. To obtain this work men had to queue for long hours at employment exchanges. The work itself is, of course, dirty and laborious.

An NEDO survey (1975) at about the same time showed that a full-time kitchen hand was in the lowest 13 per cent of earners in all industries and services. Half of them were in the category of 'low-paid' workers (compared with 11 per cent in the rest of industry).

It is apparent from these studies that poverty (even when defined in relation to the narrow government standard of a minimum income rather than 'a lack of resources which include the whole range of services and benefits provided by central and local government' (Sinfield 1969: 58)) has remained a serious problem during the post-war period. Indeed, a number of factors (in particular, the disproportionate increase in the numbers of the elderly) seem likely to result in pressures towards greater inequality (Townsend 1975). Such deprivation emphasizes the need to consider destitution in a wider context and to regard critically theories that equate poverty with maladjustment or deficiency of personality. It would, however, be misleading to define poverty solely in terms of a low income. Deprivation, of the kind recorded by Townsend and others, often reflects a variety of unmet needs for particular social and medical services which, in conjunction with an adequate income, would enable individuals to cope 'optimally' with problems not experienced by the majority of the population. The special needs of the elderly provide an example. The Welfare State, however, based on a system of social security essentially geared to the average needs of the 'normal' working population (i.e. to 'consistent contributors' (M. Brown 1969)), has frequently been deficient in making appropriate provision in cases of minority need. In consequence, disadvantages resulting from illness, handicap, infirmity, and atypical social relationships have persisted. Often, one disadvantage is related to others. Wilder, for example, found that of 174 schizophrenic patients followed up after discharge from an East London Hospital, a third were living in sub-standard housing and half were unemployed. The multiplicity of deprivations that such groups experience result in their members living what has been termed a 'second-class mode of life' (Butterworth and Holman 1975: 79).

Such disadvantaged, minority groups may be called 'outsiders', employing the term given prominence in a rather different context, by Becker (1963). The term is used in two senses. It implies first, the existence of needs which are not experienced by the majority of the population, and second, that the reaction of the state to groups possessing these needs will tend to emphasize their separate, minority status. The statutory response reflects, in some respects, Pinker's concept of social and spatial 'distance' (1971). The social remoteness of the poor, he suggests, can make their deprivations less real, especially in cases where isolation is increased by admission to an institution. 'Once groups like the aged and mentally handicapped are isolated they are both more easily forgotten and made aware of their stigmatized identity . . .' (Pinker 1971: 173). According to this view an inverse relationship exists between the distance of the recipient from the receiver and motivation to provide adequate services. Groups possessing special needs become victims of their minority status.

The problems experienced by these groups have elements in

common which result from the low priority they are given by the social and medical services. The provision made for them is deficient in quantity and quality, its inadequacy sometimes exacerbating the situation of clients. Some homeless families placed in large blocks of institutional Part III accommodation, for example, find their address an obstacle to finding work (Sinfield 1969). Nor (since 'outsiders' often possess several needs which may not fall neatly within departmental boundaries) is provision adequately co-ordinated. At the very least, Brown commented, it should be ensured 'that the policies of [local authority] departments are not in conflict with each other and there is some sharing of information about what is going on' (M. J. Brown 1974: 241). A further area where greater co-operation is needed is between the personal social services and the health authorities.

The problems arising from uncoordinated services, and the recognition of deficiences in the standard and nature of statutory provision, have resulted in voluntary organizations assuming an important role in meeting the needs of 'outsiders'. These organizations have seen themselves as pioneering bodies whose function, in special cases of need, is to innovate (Nightingale 1973). In practice, however, because of the deficiencies in provision we have discussed, they have come to be occupied mainly in 'gap-filling'. This tendency has reflected the lack of variety as well as the insufficiency of the statutory services.

These points can most clearly be conveyed by considering the situation of particular groups. We will therefore discuss some of the problems confronting two groups of 'outsiders'; one-parent families and the physically disabled. Although the specific needs of these groups differ and their situation might, at first sight, appear to have little in common with the problems of destitute people, the difficulties facing each group have a common aetiology. Each possesses atypical needs requiring special provision. Each, for reasons already discussed, lacks adequate financial help and supportive services. In this respect their situation reflects that of other disadvantaged minorities such as the elderly and the mentally ill.

It is estimated that there are about 730,000 one-parent families with 1.25 million children (Turner 1978). Services for this group are insufficient to meet their needs, especially after the birth of the child (Sainsbury 1977). Their main requirements are for an adequate level of income and counselling concerning financial entitlements and negotiations with the courts. The 1974 Finer Report recommended a new non-contributory benefit, the Guaranteed Maintenance Allowance, which would have involved a fairly substantial payment to single parents plus an allowance for each child according to means (Committee on One-Parent Families 1974). This proposal was not accepted by the government. In an article published four years after Finer, Turner said of the Committee's recommendations: 'It was all too much. More than half the report's 230 recommendations have been rejected outright. Its two major proposals – guaranteed maintenance allowance (GMA) and family courts – have been rejected as too complex and too expensive' (Turner 1978: 11). Marsden (1969), in a survey of fatherless families on national assistance, found that, within this group, unmarried mothers were particularly disadvantaged. They had incomes below the average for the whole group, stemming from a lack of help from relatives, an inability to work due to young children and, in some cases, a reduction in assistance because of suspected cohabitation. Two-thirds lived in poor quality rented housing for which they paid higher than average rents. Three-quarters were overcrowded compared with one in ten of all households in England and Wales. Many complained of a lack of help and of censorious and unsympathetic attitudes from Social Security and local authority officials. 'Some of the families', Marsden commented, 'had been homeless or had suffered other severe hardships before strong backing from social workers or doctors had got them a house. Even so, the families tended to be rehoused in the roughest areas on the worst estates' (Marsden 1969: 212). At present, voluntary self-help action groups like Gingerbread form a major source of support and advice for this group.

The hardship and frustration that one-parent families experience as a result of inadequate financial help and a lack of supportive services is reflected in the situation of the physically disabled. In a 1977 publication, the Disability Alliance estimated that between 0.8 and 0.9 million of the 1.2 million disabled people in Britain were living in poverty or on its margins. Disability rapidly resulted in deprivation. Maclean and Jefferys (1974), who surveyed an unselected sample of patients with paraplegia or tetraplegia, demonstrated substantial impoverishment due to loss of earning power, reduced facilities for leisure activities and problems in relation to transport and housing. In some cases, a decline in earning power was accompanied by the need for increased expenditure. Hyman showed that extra expenditure on diet, clothing, heating, laundry, telephone, and supplies from the chemist were incurred at an average of £65 a year by a disabled group of working age (Shearer 1977). Very few qualified for supplementary allowances for these items. When they did the money allowed was inadequate to the need.

Those advocating more comprehensive provision for the physically disabled have emphasized the need to differentiate clearly between the category of short-term sickness on the one hand and permanent disablement on the other. Hunt commented:

> 'At the moment, someone in bed for a week with flu may receive virtually the same insurance benefit as someone facing a life-time of total paralysis, or dying slowly of cancer. It is obvious that Sickness Benefit and other allowances are scaled, even with earnings-related supplements, simply to tide people over limited periods off work, not for years of disablement' (Hunt 1973: 111–2).

He pointed out that deficiencies in provision affected some disabled groups particularly severely, citing those physically and mentally handicapped men and women (about 150,000 people) who either had never been employed or whose contribution record did not qualify them for insurance benefits. The prospect facing this group was subsistence on supplementary benefits. The majority were unmarried and many lacked family support.

In a study of the prevalence and nature of physical disability in Tower Hamlets, Skinner (1969) concluded that the amenities provided by the borough did not compensate for the effects of disability and a lack of close social ties. The extent of amenity deficiency experienced by the handicapped persons who were interviewed compared unfavourably with that in the borough population as a whole. His findings in relation to housing suggested that the personal needs of handicapped persons applying for local authority accommodation had little effect in weighting their claim. The housing procedure was for urgent medical priority to be awarded to applicants by nomination of the medical officer but, during 1967, only forty-four such recommendations were made out of a total of 650 applications. There was no evidence of specifically designed accommodation for physically handicapped persons being available, or that plans for such units were being considered. Much of the pressure for an improvement of these conditions comes from the Disablement Income Group, a nationwide voluntary organization founded in 1965 by two housewives disabled by multiple sclerosis.

We have not attempted a comprehensive consideration of the situation and problems of one-parent families and the physically disabled. Our aim has been rather to draw attention to some common features of their situation – in particular, that each group has atypical needs which result (given the deficiencies of provision for minority groups) in substantial deprivation. This deprivation leads to dependency. Since the position of dependents in our culture is usually seen as inferior, stigma is imposed on the groups in question (Forder 1966). The less likely the recovery prospects the greater the likelihood that this will occur (Pinker 1971). Since the ability of groups to reject the low status ascribed to them is a function of power, 'outsiders' like the elderly, the physically handicapped, and one-parent families are unlikely successfully to challenge the low esteem in which they are held so as to produce changes in their situation. As Pinker comments of the elderly: 'They lack both the political and physical power to demand a greater economic reward for past services, none of which are viewed as exceptional and all of which have already been evaluated retrospectively in market terms. Over their working lifetime they have become habituated to a place of lowly social esteem. . . . The facts of relative poverty will reinforce the sense of social distance from prospective givers, as will their high propensity for institutionalization. The physically and mentally handicapped will be still more adversely affected by these factors' (Pinker 1971: 173).

These problems have, however, been obscured by the claim of the Welfare State to be a 'universalist' service. The assumption that all in need would be provided for was associated with a failure to systematically order social priorities (despite scarce resources) or assess the relative adequacy of the provision made to different groups. A well-researched basis for what Titmuss has called 'more selective services and benefits provided, as social rights, on the basis of the *needs* of certain categories, groups and territorial areas . . . and not on the basis of individual *means*; . . .' (Titmuss 1968: 114, author's emphasis) was not constructed. In consequence, while universalism persisted as an objective, its achievement was, in practice, prevented by 'the free play of social forces' (Pinker 1971: 188). The best social services were utilized by the middle-class, 'practising positive discrimination on their own behalf. . . . The combined lack of adequate research and adequate resources has reduced universalism to the level of a slogan' (Pinker 1971: 188).

Although the relevance of this analysis to the problems of the destitute is clear enough, it is important to answer the question why most 'single parents', most elderly people, and most of the severely physically handicapped, are not, in our terms, severely destitute. The answer is that the network of benefits for particular causes of social disadvantage is usually effective enough to maintain those affected, who have no other sources of support, at least at the poverty line or just above it. Where this line should be drawn is a matter for argument but homeless families, for example, will usually receive a higher priority that 'homeless single persons'.* Women receive far more support than men and rarely become severely destitute. Nevertheless, thousands of people fall through the welfare net and find themselves in reception centres or other shelters or sleeping rough. Why, and how can it be prevented? In the following section, we shall review the main studies of destitute people carried out during the past twenty-five years.

Surveys of destitute people

There is a considerable circulation of destitute people between common lodging houses, free shelters, reception centres, and 'the streets'. In the survey of Homeless Single Persons (NAB 1966), carried out by the National Assistance Board in 1965, it was found that a quarter of those in common lodging houses had previously used reception centres and a quarter had sometimes slept rough. Of those living in reception centres, about a half had sometimes used private lodgings, three-quarters had used common lodging houses, and three-quarters had slept rough. Of those found sleeping rough, two-fifths had used common lodging houses and one-fifth reception centres. These proportions were based on the answers of the people interviewed. Nearly four-fifths (77 per cent) of the clientele had been in their present accommodation for six months or more. Commercial organizations and private owners together provided 44 per cent of all the beds. About half the men were out of work and receiving National Assistance.

P. W. Digby, who carried out the .OPCS survey of hostels and lodging houses in 1972, made similar observations (Digby 1976). Only 10 per cent of residents were women and very few of the men were young (only 11 per cent under thirty but 20 per cent sixty-five or over). Two-thirds of the men said they had never been married. Very

---

*The Housing (Homeless Persons) Act of 1977 will be discussed in Chapter 7.

few were coloured at that time (fewer than 2 per cent) but this situation could be changing (CRC 1974). One third of the men had been resident in the same place for more than two years and half had been living in the same kind of accommodation for at least ten years. Over half (54 per cent) said they had slept rough at some time in the past (14 per cent frequently) and a quarter had used reception centres (3 per cent frequently); such men were particularly likely to be living in Salvation Army Hostels. About a half of the men aged under sixty-five years were working, mostly in unskilled and casual jobs. Most of those out of work had been unemployed for at least a year. Although ill-health of various kinds was very common only 8 per cent had been admitted to psychiatric hospitals. Nearly one half had at some time been in prison.

One of the most interesting aspects of this survey concerned the attitudes of men to their accommodation. Nearly half were content where they were (recalling the institutional attitudes of long-stay residents in hospital (Wing and Brown 1970)) but half wanted to live elsewhere, particularly in a bedsitter or a flat. A desire for more privacy and greater independence was frequently mentioned.

There have been a few smaller surveys of common lodging houses in Belfast (Sargaison, 1954), Edinburgh (Priest 1971; Scott *et al*. 1966) and Glasgow (Laidlaw 1956), carried out by professional people (a hospital almoner, general practitioners, a medical officer of health, and a psychiatrist) who gave a service to the men and were appalled by the lack of treatment, care, and amenities. These studies, like those of hostels and reception centres to be reviewed later, were not intended to be more than descriptive. The sampling procedures and methods of data collection varied and none of the authors used standard techniques of diagnosis, so that the results cannot strictly be compared. The authors were not aiming at big science but to report, as factually as possible, on problems which 'authority' seemed to be ignoring. Nevertheless, the social characteristics of the men were very similar to those described in the large surveys. They tended to be single, middle-aged to elderly, and unskilled. A substantial proportion of those under sixty-five were unemployed. There was a good deal of physical frailty and disability, as would be expected because of the high proportion of elderly people, but much of it was untreated. A report on chest diseases found in destitute men in the Grassmarket area of Edinburgh was particularly important because of the wealth of detail and recommendations made (McCrory 1975). Severe psychiatric conditions and alcoholism were noted in fair proportion but the only very high figure was that of Priest who found 20 per cent of his sample had 'schizophrenia' (Priest 1971). However, only 14 per cent of Priest's sample had been admitted to psychiatric hospitals, which is not higher than expected for this age-group but falls within the range of the other lodging house surveys.

The OPCS survey showed that the largest single provider of hostels and lodging houses was the Salvation Army which was responsible for one quarter of all the beds. The larger hostels run by the Army are well-known for the fact that they do not turn away the categories noted by Wingfield-Digby as unwelcome to most establishments: 'drunkards, disruptive influences, mentally ill, disreputable, verminous, out of work' (Salvation Army 1976). Men in the OPCS survey who had often been in reception centres or who had frequently slept rough were particularly likely to be found in the large Army hostels. Lodge Patch (1970), who interviewed 123 men in two London hostels found that eighteen (15 per cent) had schizophrenia. The criteria for diagnosis were strict and the proportion is likely to have been an underestimate. Fourteen of the men had been in hospital. Another ten men were severely depressed (some of them near-suicidal) and twenty-five were heavy drinkers. Crossley and Denmark (1969), who studied another Army hostel, also found a high proportion of people with mental illness, two-thirds of whom had been in hospital.

This higher frequency of mental disability and alcoholism in Salvation Army hostels, compared with the general run of lodging houses, was matched in several studies of the Camberwell Reception Centre carried out by nurses, social workers, general practitioners, and psychiatrists (Edwards, et al. 1968; Ollendorf and Morgan 1968; Page 1964, 1965; Pritchard 1969). Griffith Edwards and his colleagues, for example, carried out a census survey of men using the centre. Apart from the usual characteristics (e.g. 80 per cent were unemployed, half of whom had been out of work for more than a year) they found that a quarter of the men said they had been in a psychiatric hospital during the previous year and another quarter described a severe alcohol problem. Other surveys (of longer-stay residents) found even higher proportions.

Edwards and his colleagues also carried out a study of men who were sleeping rough (Edwards et al. 1966), although they were self-selected in the sense that they were using a soup kitchen in Stepney. Two-thirds of them had been sleeping out for a year or more,

58 per cent were crude spirit drinkers, and 39 per cent had been admitted to psychiatric hospitals. Peter Archard (1975), from his participant observation, has written a vivid account of men in drinking schools. They used shelters on occasions and knew where the best handouts could be obtained but were rarely prepared to accept offers of longer-term accommodation. They were not 'vagrant' in the sense that they moved about the country a great deal. He emphasized that members of drinking schools, far from being 'desocialized', adopted strict social conventions dictated by their need to obtain daily supplies of alcohol and to keep out of trouble as far as possible in their public way of life.

This series of studies demonstrates the degree of overlap between men in unskilled employment who are living in poverty, men in lodging houses who are unemployed or working only casually, men in large hostels such as those run by the Salvation Army, men in reception centres, and men sleeping rough. They are all socially disadvantaged. However, the frequency and severity of physical and mental disability and alcoholism increases with severity and chronicity of destitution and is most predominant among those who are sleeping rough.

The recommendations made by authors are aimed mainly at the fact of untreated disability. Scott, Gaskell, and Morell (1966), in the light of their experience in general practice, suggested that attention could profitably be given to problems resulting from the high geographical mobility of the men, which led to difficulty in communication between out-patient departments, family doctors, and statutory and voluntary agencies. Crossley and Denmark (1969) were mainly concerned with the lack of after-care facilities for homeless patients after discharge from psychiatric hospitals and recommended 'asylum' for those who needed it. Whiteley (1970) concluded that a therapeutic community might be the best means of helping men whose predominant characteristic was social isolation – 'the common and basic factor . . . and that is what must be tackled.' The Edinburgh Grassmarket studies (Rooney and Woolf 1975) made detailed and useful recommendations about the prevention and treatment of chest disease and about making welfare benefits more easily available.

Recent research at Camberwell Reception Centre

The most thorough survey of men at Camberwell Reception Centre was commissioned by the Department of Health from the Social Psychiatry Unit and carried out by David Tidmarsh and Suzanne MacGregor Wood (Tidmarsh and Wood 1972a,b; Wood 1976, 1979). They first studied the 1968–9 casepapers in order to discover how many men used the centre, how long they stayed and some of their main characteristics. They then interviewed, in 1970–1, a sample of 'new cases', a sample of those who had attended before ('casuals') and a sample of those who were 'in residence'. In all, 381 men were interviewed. Finally, further information was obtained from other agencies concerning contacts of various kinds and subsequent referals.

During 1968, approximately 4,000 men attended the centre for the first time and 4,000 others on a second or subsequent occasion. During the period of the research between 200 and 400 beds on any given night were occupied on a temporary basis and approximately 400 more by longer-stay 'residents'. The characteristics of both groups of men were very similar to those described in earlier surveys. The investigators reviewed all the information available about each individual interviewed, on the basis of which they assessed the predominant reason for destitution. (Many people, of course, had more than one problem.) These judgements were clearly subjective and there is no means of assessing their validity but they represent an attempt at systematic assessment which deserves to be taken seriously and to be replicated independently. The results (with sampling fractions adjusted so as to represent the total yearly intake) are shown in *Table 2(1)*.

As would be expected, the 'residents' were most likely to be disabled, the 'casuals' next (including a very high proportion of alcoholics), and new attenders least. Mental illness of a fairly severe kind and alcoholism were common in all three groups and accounted for 55 per cent of the residents. If the 20 per cent of the latter group with 'personality disorders' are added (the term means no more – but no less – than poor all-round social performance over a long period of time with no obvious cause), as well as 20 per cent with physical illness or infirmity, it is evident that, in the judgement of the investigators, virtually all the residents were destitute because they were handicapped in some way.

These mainly clinical results were complemented by sociological data on the histories of the men. At the time they used the centre the men fell into three broad categories: those who habitually 'sleep

Table (2) 1:   *The predominant problems of men using the Camberwell Reception Centre*

predominant problem	new cases (number per year)		casuals (number per year)		residents (number on any night)	
mental illness	890	22%	540	14%	117	29%
alcoholism and addiction	550	14%	1,520	38%	104	26%
personality disorder	680	17%	800	20%	75	19%
pathological gambling	90	2%	140	3%	—	—
epilepsy	30	1%	70	2%	7	2%
physical illness	120	3%	230	6%	62	16%
old age	60	2%	70	2%	7	2%
migrant workers	60	2%	120	3%	—	—
job problem	1,150	28%	420	10%	14	3%
situational	370	9%	90	2%	14	3%
TOTALS	4,000	100%	4,000	100%	400	100%

rough', living on handouts and the proceeds of begging and scavenging (17 per cent of new arrivals, 28 per cent of those admitted repeatedly, and no fewer than 39 per cent of those who stay on at the centre as 'residents'); those who live a life of poverty and insecurity, without a real home of their own or security of employment, and who are rapidly precipitated into destitution by any crisis in their lives (16 per cent, 32 per cent and 31 per cent); and low-paid workers who are often in transit between jobs and accommodation but who merge into the larger group of men in unskilled and semi-skilled manual occupations (67 per cent, 40 per cent, 30 per cent).

The social background of all these groups has one predominant characteristic: 'a general lack of any advantage or privilege that would facilitate the acquisition and maintenance of a recognised position in society'. The following description pertains to the group as a whole rather than to individuals but it gives a fair picture of their lives. They tend to come from large families housed in poor and overcrowded conditions, and their fathers were often unskilled manual workers. They achieved little at school, truanted a good deal, and acquired few vocational skills. They were at a disadvantage compared with their siblings. On leaving school they found themselves in an area where unemployment was high, particularly in unskilled occupations, and where it was difficult to find cheap accommodation away from home. Many moved to other cities in search of work. During their twenties, they did not, like most of their contemporaries, marry and have children. Instead they tended to move from job to job in single-sex trades, cut off from the rest of society. Kitchen portering was probably the single commonest job. Some were in the armed forces. They tended not to save money or to contribute to pension schemes, and were quickly out of pocket when they became unemployed, and so had to accept social security. A very high proportion had criminal records, particularly offences connected with alcoholism and vagrancy.

Even when working at their best, many of these men were living in a financially precarious situation and the accidents of life, together with drinking or gambling, could easily move them towards real destitution. Their first contact with the reception centre was made, on average, in their mid-thirties, and for some this was the first of many visits. Since then, the average age at which destitution first occurs has probably decreased, and there are more young people sleeping rough or using shelters (Diamond 1972; WECVS 1976).

Although this was not a longitudinal study, and although the details of each individual's experience will differ, it seems reasonable to speak of a 'characteristic' career pattern followed, with modifications, by a large proportion of men who become destitute. One of the modifications is, of course, the onset of physical or mental illness. Tidmarsh and Wood suggested that such an onset is often associated with a sharp decline in social performance. Most of the mentally ill men, for example, were living in a family setting before the time of first admission to hospital. Other studies have shown that people with schizophrenia tend to move out of a family setting, both before and after the onset (Gerard and Houston 1953; Hare 1956). Severe alcoholism is a different kind of complication and a very common one.

One of the central recommendations made by the research team to the Department was that more sheltered hostel accommodation should be made available, by hospitals, by local authorities and, in large conurbations such as London, by a special organization with a specific interest in homeless handicapped people – not only in reception centres, although this is where most clients would come from initially, but in prisons, hospitals and common lodging houses. It was thought that the Department itself should accept this last responsibility, at least until the new service was well under way. Another recommendation was that shelters should be established for those who were unwilling to accept any other form of care, perhaps by voluntary organizations subsidized by the Department. Since it was not possible to lay down cut and dried specifications concerning provision, the team also suggested that any substantial innovations in services should be independently evaluated.

The need for further research

This survey of post-war studies demonstrates that identifiable groups with a higher than average risk of impoverishment are not receiving as much help as they need or as it was planned they would receive when the policies of the welfare state were being formulated. It is difficult, in any particular instance, to show evidence that destitution would in fact have been reduced further than it has been if social policies had been different. Nevertheless, in the fields of housing, employment, and handicap the presumption must be strong. We would not argue such a high presumption for the effectiveness of techniques of income-maintenance or of concentrating resources in deprived geographical areas though they might be useful for other purposes. Most poor people do not, in fact, live in deprived areas and many of the destitute people who do have come from elsewhere.

The fact that these are highly complex questions does not mean that no further light can be thrown on them. For example, a variety of longitudinal studies, such as those of Douglas (1968) in the field of education, would be likely to prove fruitful. The problems of adolescents in a high-unemployment society also merit detailed attention, as the Court Report suggested (Committee on Child Health Services 1976).

However, it is clear that destitution, even the severe and chronic destitution which is our main concern, is likely to remain a problem for the foreseeable future. It has been suggested, given scarce resources, that an interest in helping the destitute defeats its own object since it detracts from the priority that ought to be given to primary prevention. This view has usually been put by those who regard an interest in the medical as well as the social aspects of destitution as counter-productive. We do not think they have made their case.

A more cogent objection was expressed in the title of an article by David Donnison (1971) – 'No More Reports'. The point he was making is a fair one. There is now a great deal of descriptive detail about homeless single people and homeless families. Many recommendations have been put forward, some of them so obvious that they hardly needed research to justify them. What is needed is action. Of course, we agree.

There are, however, four reasons why it is necessary to undertake further research into methods of helping chronically destitute people, in spite of the fact that recommendations based on earlier work have not been acted upon. In the first place, a long gestation period has usually followed even discoveries and developments of clear-cut merit in the field of commercial technology. There are no parallel discoveries in the social sciences and no-one can be sure how rapidly research results should be applied. Even if there were a specific conclusion of immediate apparent applicability, however, a second issue arises, which is that of the relationship between research and reform. No doubt many research workers, whatever their field, are motivated by the expectation that their work will eventually be put into practice. Nevertheless, curiosity and the provision of new knowledge are also powerful motivating forces. To the extent that research workers sacrifice the latter to the former motivation they are likely to be pressing an interpretation of their results that fits a particular philosophical or ideological view, and may thereby miss the truth of the matter. This leads to the third point, which is that research workers are often wrong in their conclusions, or in their interpretation of them. Knowledge improves when theories are made to compete with each other before educated public opinion and, eventually, though the process may be a long one, false theories are eliminated. It is scientifically unsound, as well as arrogant, to imagine that other workers cannot improve on one's own efforts, or on those of colleagues whose results one approves. A diversity of approaches is essential. The fourth reason is social rather than scientific. Sometimes, research needs to be carried out in order to redirect attention to solutions that other workers have already discovered, in order to bring them again to public attention. We do not think this is usually a sufficient motivation for research but it is not negligible as an extra reason for undertaking a study.

David Brandon's attractive-sounding question 'If we knew the answer to this question, would it really make any difference to homeless people?', is not a sure guide (Brandon 1975). Very few hypotheses derivable from the theories of destitution outlined earlier have been empirically tested; indeed, one could say that scientific work in this field has hardly begun. A good deal of ground clearing remains. Even in the more immediately practical area of 'rehabilitation and resettlement' we cannot draw a more solid conclusion from earlier work than that present efforts are unsatisfactory. Our own interest lies in this latter field and we are in no doubt that there is more work to be done.

Ideas about rehabilitation should be derived from knowledge of two fundamental questions. One concerns the expectations of the individual and people in his immediate social environment. The other concerns the factors that hinder the achievement of these expectations. These are of three kinds: (a) intrinsic impairments, as in the case of severe mental retardation, epilepsy, physical disability, or the impairments that accompany chronic schizophrenia; (b) extrinsic disadvantages, such as a lack of education, family support, or vocational and social skills; (c) the individual's response to these impairments and disadvantages if this, in itself, is handicapping, showing itself in lowered self-confidence or self-esteem, and a lack of motivation to achieve a level of performance that is actually within reach. These responses depend a great deal on the image reflected back to the individual from his social environment.

These three types of handicapping factor interact to produce the unique pattern of social disablement found in any given individual. Techniques of rehabilitation can be directed at any of the components of disablement, or at improving assets or compensating for handicaps. One technique that has had some success is trying to improve self-confidence, or trying to demonstrate work skills that the individual thought he did not possess. This, very often, is an attempt to undo harm that has previously been done. Other techniques include the acquisition of new social skills. Very little work of this kind has been attempted with destitute men.

The aim of rehabilitation (or habilitation) is resettlement (or settlement), but it is useful to conceptualize this aim in terms of three ladders; vocational, domestic, and social. The same individual may be able to make more progress in one of these three areas than in the others, and he may never climb to the top of any of the ladders. The provision of a range of sheltered environments would ensure that people could find a degree of security at the appropriate level, even if they did not reach full competence in all three areas. It would also ensure that hard-won progress was not lost. Some people, however, are so severely handicapped, or have so little motivation to change, that very little progress can be expected at all. It is no help to them to be unthinkingly optimistic about the likely effects of rehabilitation.

Summary

In spite of the series of post-war measures designed to perfect the system of benefits and supports known as the Welfare State, poverty and other forms of social disadvantage have persisted. There are many reasons for this. Unemployment has not been prevented; indeed, it now appears more and more to be a long-term feature of industrialized societies. The lowest paid workers, i.e. those in casual unskilled jobs, have not improved their position relative to the rest. The benefits given to groups of people with 'single disadvantages' (one-parent families, the physically disabled, the elderly) have not kept pace with inflation. Expenditure on the National Health Service, and on local authority Social Service Departments, has not resulted in the prevention of disability or social deviance. People exposed to one type of disadvantage tend to accumulate others, notably because they become stigmatized and lose status. The emphasis on 'single solutions' has led to a multiplicity of agencies, each dealing with one type of disadvantage, and thus to the possibility that multiply disadvantaged people will fail to receive adequate help from any of them. Those least able to 'work the system' are most likely to become destitute.

Studies of men who use common lodging houses and hostels for 'homeless single people' show that they are predominantly middle-aged and elderly, out of touch with their families, unskilled, and in casual work or unemployed. Social disadvantage was also characteristic of residents of the large hostels of the Salvation Army, users of reception centres and shelters, and those who slept rough. The frequency and severity of physical and mental disability and alcoholism increased with severity and chronicity of destitution and was most evident among those sleeping rough.

The next four chapters are devoted to an assessment of two contrasting types of service, each attempting to cope with the problems of severely destitute men.

3 Aims and design
of the research

Aims

The research to be described in this book arose directly from the survey of Camberwell Reception Centre described in Chapter 2. The recommendations made concerning the range of shelters, hostels and workshops needed by the destitute were not, in fact, implemented, although other plans (to be considered in Chapter 6) were formulated, intended to allow the eventual closure of Camberwell. The voluntary movement also moved forward, one of the most substantial organizations being the St Mungo Community Trust, the origins of which were described in Chapter 1. By May 1972, this organization administered thirteen houses ('communities'), operated a nightly soup run and other services, and employed some twenty-five full-time workers. In common with other members of the new voluntary movement, St Mungo's claimed that their informal approach was likely to be more successful than that of the statutory services. The Department of Health, impressed by these claims, decided to make a substantial annual grant to the Trust to allow it to maintain and expand its activities, on condition that the effectiveness of its services was independently evaluated. The Social Psychiatry Unit accepted a commission to carry out this evaluation.

Hyman defined the purpose of evaluation as providing 'objective, systematic and comprehensive evidence on the degree to which the program achieves its intended objectives' (Hyman *et al.* 1962: 5). This is the minimum that should be attempted, even if the aims of the organization are so clear-cut as to present specific criteria against which achievement can be judged. If an agency's aims are ambiguous or vague, or if there is some conflict between leaders as to what they are, or if actual practice is inconsistent with stated policy, the research team has a much more active task. We consider (Wing 1972) that it is, in principle, necessary for research workers to clarify and test not only the overt aims of the agency but also any 'aims' that seem implicit in its organization and practice. This principle is particularly important in so-called 'action research' since one of its useful consequences may be to help the agency redefine its objectives.

We had three broad research interests: the assessment of new techniques of rehabilitation and resettlement (or new modifications of old techniques), the evaluation of policy changes made on the basis of research results ('action research'), and the comparison of statutory and voluntary approaches. These interests were considerably wider than the straightforward evaluation of effectiveness required by the commission but neither St Mungo's nor the Department demurred during preliminary discussions. This is not the place to consider the more general problems of commissioned research but it should be mentioned that, during six years of work at St Mungo's and in several reception centres, we never, at any time, felt under pressure to adopt any particular research design or method, and received only helpful comments on the way we had interpreted and written up the results. We were always free to reject these comments and the final formulation of the studies is entirely òur responsibility.

Action research

The three research aims were pursued in parallel rather than in sequence but the action research determined the timing of the comparative and observational studies. We shall therefore begin with an outline of this.

St Mungo's had as its major aim the rehabilitation and resettlement of destitute men through the use of a 'primary' means of contact (the soup run) where food was offered free and without conditions, and the offer of a place in a community house if, as a result of contact on the soup run, a man expressed a wish for it. The experience in the house (together with more conventional forms of help and contact with other agencies) was believed to be 'therapeutic', enabling many men to move to more independent accommodation. This sequence was presented as a contrast to the authoritarian 'processing' thought to be characteristic of statutory services, where contacts tended merely to emphasize still further the man's alienation from society and to offer no hope of rehabilitation.

Our initial research aims, therefore, were: first, to discover whether the St Mungo workers did induce men on the streets to enter the houses and accept help; second, to estimate what proportion were able to settle in one of the houses; third, to find out what happened after they left. If there was, indeed, a degree of success in resettlement, a fourth aim was to describe what sort of men benefitted and what features of the regime seemed especially beneficial. Lesser degrees of success, such as a decrease in handicaps or an improvement in well-being, could also be measured.

It was assumed that these aims would be pursued in stages. On the completion of the first phase of evaluation, tentative conclusions would be drawn and communicated to the Director and staff, who would then have the option of altering their procedures. Another phase of evaluation, with the same aims as before, would then begin. Thus the research would proceed in cycles of evaluation, policy change, re-evaluation, and further policy change, until little further progress seemed likely. This was the essence of the 'action research' approach.

Marris and Rein (1967) suggested that policy making

'concentrates upon the next step,. breaking the sequence into discrete, manageable decisions. . . . The shorter the span of action under review, the less we do not know, and the quicker we shall discover the wisdom of our decisions. Hence it is much easier to make rational choices if a plan of action is broken down to a series of proximate steps, and the plan is open to revision as each step is completed' (Marris and Rein 1967: 204).

The recommendations of the research team were therefore presented in discrete packages, each separated by a period of time during which any innovations could be evaluated.

Experience of larger-scale action research projects in this country had not been altogether encouraging. The two major studies were the Educational Priority Area project (Halsey 1973) designed to evaluate some of the proposals (concerning education in deprived areas) put forward by the Plowden Committee (DES 1967), and the Community Development Project (Lees and Smith 1975), based mainly at the Home Office, which employed an action research strategy in neighbourhoods identified as having high social needs. These programmes were based on the belief that social science and social policy should be closely interrelated. The role of research was to identify problems, to participate in developing policies to meet them, and to evaluate the effectiveness of these policies. This implied a relatively novel assumption – that political ends could be pursued by social science experiment. As one observer of the process commented: 'The new idea acknowledges ignorance. The politician commits himself to trying a plan in an experimentally devised situation, but at the same time commits himself to abandoning it for another scheme if evaluation by the most valid social science techniques shows that it does not work' (Halsey 1970: 251).

The difficulties faced by 'experimental social administration' of this kind were considerable. On the one hand, experience was to suggest that a co-operative relationship between social scientists and policymakers could not always be achieved. The different time-scales of university and government decision making and the divergent tendencies of academic research and policy (one general, the other more specific) created problems in establishing mutually acceptable working relationships. On the other hand, the process of evaluating social action posed considerable technical problems. As Halsey remarked:

'The laboratory [in which action research takes place] is, by definition, natural and not experimental. There are political as well as scientific determinants of the localities chosen for the projects. The desired outcomes of action are often imprecisely defined and in any case resistant to clear measurement. The inputs are not completely controlled and the relation between input and output is to that extent indeterminate. It is doubtful whether the intellectual tools of social scientists are adequate to the task' (Halsey 1970: 251).

A recognition of these problems (and the appreciation that action research was unlikely to provide policy recommendations validated by controlled experiment) did not result in a diminution of enthusiasm for this approach. Instead some proponents of action research suggested that its proper role was one of general exploration in areas where little research had been undertaken, with a view to establishing tentative hypotheses concerning the costs and benefits of change. 'Far from providing cut and dried answers,' one researcher concluded, 'evaluation . . . must in most cases serve to heighten the problems of choice: there are no "solutions". . . .' Nor, it was believed, were 'solutions' of much use in areas where major policy initiatives were required. 'The dilemma is that almost by definition areas of social life where there is the leisure and stability to test out options in a systematic way, will tend to be those of specialist rather than general importance' (Lees and Smith 1975: 198).

We were not as convinced of the value of 'general exploration' nor of the impossibility of using experimental design as some of these authors. We were prepared to adopt the most rigorous design compatible with obtaining new knowledge, which meant, of course, taking into account the attitudes of those we were working with and the constraints under which they were themselves working. It will be seen that in the event, the use of control groups was hardly necessary, so that the question of feasibility did not arise.

A detailed account of the methods used will be given as each phase of the research is described.

Phases of the research programme and presentation of the results

A brief account of the research programme is given here in order to clarify the presentation of results in the next three chapters. It may be found useful to refer back to this chronology while reading these chapters.

(1) Pilot phase at St Mungo's (September 1971–June 1972)   A pilot study was conducted during this period in order to test various methods of data collection and allow a preliminary description of the characteristics of St Mungo residents and workers. The main technique used was participant observation. At that time there were four houses (known as Group I) serving men referred from the soup run; these comprised an assessment house and three other hostels. The thirty-five men in residence on 1 January 1972 and the seventy men admitted during the

following three months formed the sample. A brief follow-up study of men leaving the houses was also carried out. The results, and the conclusions drawn from them, profoundly influenced the subsequent stages of the research.

(2) Second phase (July 1972–December 1973)   In the second phase, the studies of the pilot phase were repeated and extended using more structured methods, in order to determine the characteristics of men selected for the houses and of those who 'settled' for a period of three months or more, and also some of the characteristics and attitudes of the staff. In order to provide a comparison group, exposed to an apparently very different environment, a similar study was carried out at the Camberwell Reception Centre and its Battersea annexe, chosen because Camberwell was the main statutory agency and the largest provider of accommodation for destitute men in London.

A register of admissions to and discharges from the houses was established, starting with a census of men resident on 1 October 1972. The continued expansion of the organization (two groups of houses and a night shelter were added), was monitored in this way. A running check was kept on the whereabouts of men admitted during specified periods of time.

(3) Third phase (January 1974–March 1976)   During the third phase, the information collected on admitted men was improved and standardized, the register of admissions was maintained, and a check was kept on the follow-up status of the groups of men identified in the second phase.

In an attempt to suggest means of helping men to settle longer in houses, a survey of reasons for leaving was carried out. Information was obtained about a group of sixty-four men who left St Mungo houses during October and November 1974, about half of whom were interviewed. On the basis of the results, it was decided to initiate an assessment exercise, in January 1975, which continued for a year. All men in groups I and II who had stayed longer than a month were considered, in order to make a crude classification of their social and drinking behaviour and to construct a simple plan for helping each one. A routine admissions procedure, based on this exercise, was adopted in November 1975.

(4) Fourth phase (April–September 1976)   In the fourth phase, a survey

was made of all men resident in three groups of houses at the end of April 1976, and of all staff working in the Community during March, 1976. The questions asked were identical to those in the interviews of 1972–3. Register data were available up to September 1976.

(5) Fifth Phase (April 1977–March 1978)   Following the completion of the main work at St Mungo's, it was decided that many of the conclusions arising from the research could be further tested by an investigation of two small reception centres that had been recently set up in London.

The criteria and results of the evaluation of the effectiveness of the St Mungo services are described in Chapter 4, together with a narrative account of the action research. Chapter 5 contains an account of the ideological changes that occurred at St Mungo's during the period of the research. Some initial comparisons between St Mungo's and the Camberwell Reception Centre are described in Chapter 6, followed by a discussion of the impact of change at St Mungo's and then by a description of two of the new small reception centres. Chapter 6 is concluded by a description of a study of destitute men observed at a number of locations in the West End of London. The material in these chapters is not presented in chronological order since this would be confusing to the reader. In Chapter 7 the results given in the preceding three chapters are discussed, in the light of the issues raised in Chapters 1 and 2.

4 The effectiveness of
a voluntary service
for helping destitute men

In the first part of this chapter a narrative account is given of the stages of the action research and of the recommendations (eight in all) that were made on the basis of the research results. Policy changes resulting from these recommendations (and from other changes, largely resulting from the expansion of services) are also described so that Part I contains a chronological account of the development of the St Mungo services which can be compared with the story of ideological development given in Chapter 5.

Part II is concerned with the criteria and assessment of overall effectiveness, i.e. with the question of settlement and resettlement. In Part III, and in the Appendix, a more detailed description is given of the living arrangements of disabled men who had 'settled' in two St Mungo houses and how workers coped with their disabilities.

Part I   The stages of action research

Methods used during the action research

Before any research work began it was thought desirable, by St Mungo staff and the research team, that the latter should spend some time attempting to become partially assimilated into Community life. One member of the team, a psychiatrist (JS), spent September to December 1971 working regularly on the soup run, joining in the activities of the Community and generally becoming a familiar part of the background. A social scientist (JL) spent December in the same way and by the time the pilot study began they felt fully accepted by both residents and staff.

Since the Community set out to provide a less institutional and structured environment than common lodging-houses and reception centres, St Mungo staff regarded formal interviewing of their residents as harmful. It was agreed, therefore, before the pilot stage, that data should be collected informally in the course of day to day interactions with the residents; information emerging from casual conversations would be subsequently recorded on to schedules. Two such schedules were used in the pilot study.

The first of these recorded demographic information about each person for whom information was required. The research team and St Mungo staff worked together to collect these data. The second questionnaire was used only by a psychiatrist and was always completed following an informal discussion with a resident. A medical and psychiatric history was obtained where possible and ratings were made of the residents' attitudes to various aspects of their life and of their 'realism and constructiveness'. A psychiatric assessment of the residents' mental state was made and diagnostic categories recorded. Full use was made of probation reports, hospital letters, and other documents. Less formal observations were also made by the research team, on the soup run, at St Mungo meetings, and during day to day life in St Mungo houses, in order to compose, as far as possible, a complete picture of the Community.

Difficulties arose because of the necessity to collect information as informally as possible. In the event, the informal method used – that of recording whatever pertinent data the resident offered in the course of conversations – was unsuccessful at two levels. First, data were fragmented and incomplete; second, there arose a degree of ambiguity concerning the role of the research workers. Residents in the houses were told that the team were carrying out research and were in the houses to observe how St Mungo's functioned. This occasionally led, however, to residents becoming anxious as to whether the results would be used to suggest that certain men were not suitable for residence.

Because of this the research workers reviewed their methods and a decision was reached to attempt more formal techniques of collecting information, including formal interviews, while accepting that these would have to cease if they were seen to be upsetting the men. The reverse, in fact, turned out to be true in most cases. Men appeared to enjoy talking about themselves and to like the privacy of a formal interview. St Mungo workers were always asked before an interview took place whether they thought it wise to see the man in question, and their advice was followed. If a man appeared at all doubtful or worried when approached by one of the research team, the interview was not carried out. The number of people not seen was very few, and throughout the period of research no cases occurred of men leaving the Community because an interview had upset them.

From the beginning of the second phase of research, formal interviewing was employed as the main method of obtaining comprehensive personal information. In order to supplement such information, a statistical register was set up and began operating on 1 October 1972. In it were recorded details of all admissions to and discharges from St Mungo houses. The statistics given in a subsequent section of this chapter are derived from this register.

The research sociologist (JL) kept a diary throughout the course of the work, in which a record was made of conversations with workers and residents, men met on the soup run, or professional visitors to the houses. Written documents, such as the minutes of the weekly meetings, were also collected.

The pilot phase

The pilot study had two main objectives:

(1) To discover whether the resettlement of destitute men in independent accommodation was being achieved.* This could

* By 'own' or 'independent' accommodation we refer to private accommodation such as flats, bedsitters and 'digs'. In a few cases residents went to live with relatives or friends

be investigated by a 'follow-up' study, to find out what happened after men left the houses.
(2) To describe the characteristics of the residents so as to assess their needs.

The pilot study was carried out during the first three months of 1972. The thirty-five men in residence in the four DHSS funded houses (comprising an 'assessment centre' and three associated houses) on 1 January 1972, and the seventy men admitted during the following three months formed the sample. A check on the whereabouts of men resident at the beginning of January, or admitted during February, was made during the first week of May, thus allowing a minimum of two months' follow-up. Very few of these men were thought to have become resettled because of their contact with St Mungo's (see p. 77).

Characteristics of the men

The characteristics of these men were not greatly different from those observed by other investigators and summarized in Chapter 2. The following data relate to the 105 men in the pilot study. Data collected during the second phase of research (on men admitted to houses during the period 1 October 1972 to 28 February 1973) were used as a check on the data collected during the pilot phase, and for a comparison of men staying in the houses for more or for less than three months. The characteristics of the two surveyed groups were very similar. A further survey was carried out in April 1976. A summary of the findings of the subsequent survey is given in *Table 4(6)* on page 85.

Age   Just under a third of the men in the houses were under forty years of age, nearly half were aged between forty and fifty-nine and a fifth were aged sixty or more. It was subsequently noted by the research team that, among residents who stayed for more than three months in the houses, 71 per cent were aged fifty or more, compared with 48 per cent of those who left houses within three months.

and this, too (if the accommodation was of the kind specified above), was classed as 'independent'. Residence in lodging houses, shelters, other supportive hostels, and reception centres was not considered to be 'resettlement' since (although providing a roof) such accommodation did not, in most cases, represent a change in the mens' previous life-style.

Birthplace   Only a third of the residents for whom information was available (N=93) had been born in London or the south of England. The same proportion (35 per cent) was born in Scotland or Ireland and 6 per cent were born abroad. The rest of the residents were born in the north of England. Two-thirds of the 'shorter-stay' men (those leaving houses within three months) were not born in England and Wales, compared with only 23 per cent of the 'longer-stay' men.

Marital Status   Over half of the residents were single; a further third had a broken marriage, leaving only 7 per cent still married. This pattern was much the same in 'longer-stay' as in 'shorter-stay' men.

Occupation   Three-quarters of the residents had worked mainly in unskilled manual work and only two out of 105 residents were known to have been employed in any kind of skilled work during the three months before their admission to a house. Two-thirds of the residents had had some kind of work during the year prior to their admission to a house, even if only briefly. There was no difference in these respects between 'shorter-stay' and 'longer-stay' men.

Accommodation   The residents were asked how much time, during the year prior to their admission to a house, they had spent in various types of accommodation. Only 13 per cent of the residents had spent most of the year in their own accommodation (flat, digs, with relatives), compared with 29 per cent who had spent most of the year sleeping rough. The rest of the residents had stayed in reception centres, lodging houses, hostels, hospitals and prisons. Out of the 105 residents, fifty-two (50 per cent) had stayed in the Camberwell Reception Centre at some time during the two years before their present admission to St Mungo's. There was no difference, in these respects, between 'shorter-stay' and 'long-stay' men.

Prison   Half the residents (53 per cent) said they had served a prison sentence and there seemed little difference between 'shorter-stay' and 'longer-stay' men in this respect. Recidivism, however, was commoner among 'shorter-stay' men; 28 per cent of 'shorter-stay' men said they had been to prison at least five times, compared to 15 per cent of the 'longer-stay' men.

Mental and physical illness   A psychiatrist (JS) assessed the mental state of sixty-seven out of the 105 St Mungo residents. Most of the residents not interviewed stayed for only a few days in the houses (twenty-four out of thirty-eight). The other residents were not interviewed because they refused to provide information or it appeared likely that they would find an interview upsetting. No diagnosis was given by the psychiatrist if no abnormality appeared at the time of his interview with a resident; i.e. diagnoses were not made on the basis of the resident's history alone.

Of the sixty-seven residents interviewed, thirty-seven (55 per cent) were given no formal diagnosis by the psychiatrist. One resident was suffering from schizophrenia. Depression was more common, though it was severe in only one out of the six cases so diagnosed. In this one case, however, it was probably a major cause of the resident's destitution. The depression of the other five residents appeared more likely to be reactive to destitution than to be causative of it. Severe alcoholism was present in eight residents, mild alcoholism in three,* and severe 'personality disorder' in nine. The latter term was used by the psychiatrist only as a last resort, when it appeared that factors within the resident were quite as strong as any social factors acting upon him or any social deprivation that he experienced, in accounting for the course of his life.† One resident was regarded as being mentally retarded and two suffered from epilepsy.

Many of the residents with severe psychiatric conditions had stayed in the houses for more than three months at the time of interview. In fact, out of the thirty residents given some sort of diagnosis by the psychiatrist, only twelve had stayed for less than a month in the houses, and eleven of these suffered from alcoholism or personality disorder. Thus, as at the Camberwell Reception Centre,

---

* 'Severe' and 'mild' alcoholism were distinguished by the presence or absence of typical withdrawal symptoms (e.g. morning shakes, delirium tremens), or other typical manifestations of prolonged heavy drinking (e.g. journey amnesia). Where a resident admitted to drinking crude spirits, but not to any of the symptoms mentioned above, this was designated by the psychiatrist as severe alcoholism. A resident who saw drinking as one of his problems, for which he needed help, but had none of the above problems and had never drunk crude spirits was designated by the psychiatrist as mildly alcoholic.

† It is important to enter this caveat because many people take a diagnosis of 'personality disorder' to mean simply that the diagnostician is labelling the individual's unusual way of life. If that were so, most destitute men would be given the diagnosis. In fact, many psychiatrists attempt to avoid the term so far as they can. See the summary relating to Mr Barnard, in the appendix, for an example of a resident considered by the psychiatrist to have a 'personality disorder'.

the more handicapped men tended to stay in residence for fairly long periods. Mental illness, however, was not as common among the St Mungo residents as among many of the destitute groups described in Chapter 2; only one resident was thought by the psychiatrist to have become destitute because of mental illness.

Serious physical illness was quite common among the residents. Of sixty-six residents for whom information was available to the psychiatrist, twenty-four (36 per cent) had had a serious physical illness during the year prior to their admission to a house, usually respiratory. Varicose veins, ankle oedema, and such like 'conditions of vagrancy' were also common. There was no tendency for residents who had been physically ill to stay longer in houses than the rest.

It was apparent from the interviews that most of the men entering St Mungo houses had a long history of social disadvantage. Many were born in areas of social and economic deprivation, acquired few vocational skills and migrated from their birthplace to areas of greater job opportunity. Their occupational history was unsettled and often spent in single-sex, casual work. Most had never married; partly, perhaps, because they found it difficult to form any kind of settled home in the midst of continual poverty and occasional unemployment. The great majority had spent most of the year before admission to a house sleeping rough or in lodging houses, reception centres, and shelters for the destitute. As well as being socially disadvantaged some men were also handicapped by physical or psychiatric disabilities and alcoholism. These findings, and the outcome of the follow-up enquiries, resulted in the first four research recommendations of the project.

It was apparent from the pilot study that the men who used St Mungo houses came from the same 'circuit' as those who used reception centres and other types of accommodation available to destitute men. Half of the St Mungo residents had used Camberwell Reception Centre during the two years before admission to a house. Most men admitted to the houses stayed for a very short time and then returned to the sort of life they had been living before. About two-thirds remained in touch with St Mungo's, usually through the soup run.

The first four recommendations

The first four recommendations were derived from the observation that St Mungo's was not succeeding in resettling destitute men in independent accommodation (see p. 77). The findings were discussed with the St Mungo management and a modification of aims agreed. The research team suggested that the central functions of St Mungo's should be two-fold. In the first place there was the purely humanitarian function of supplying food and shelter to people who lacked them. This should clearly be continued, the more so since it allowed the second function to be carried out. This was to help destitute men settle for long periods in St Mungo houses. It would mean an increase in the medium-term and longer-term accommodation provided and a lesser emphasis on the rapid turn-over of destitute men.

Our recommendations were based upon this formulation. The role of the Director would clearly be crucial. He would need to preserve the original democratic small group ideal, to preside over the enlargement of the Community, and the introduction of more formal administrative and professional methods, and to continue a pioneering role, since there were many further innovations to be made in this field.

A major implication of the formulation was that the flow of men through the assessment centre would be slower, but that a higher proportion of men would be transferred from the centre to the medium-stay houses. This required better selection of men from the soup run, which in turn required higher quality work there, and some alternative system for helping those who would benefit from a purely temporary shelter. Increasing the acceptance rate of men into the houses would require an expansion of this type of accommodation, and a more immediate pressure to set up permanent houses as well. However, it would be important to see these long-term houses (which might consist largely of bed-sitter accommodation) as developing naturally out of the present chain of St Mungo services. There were already many men who could be transferred but it was not clear what the extent of the demand would be. The priority should therefore be on more rapid expansion of medium-term accommodation, while the longer-term situation should be kept under review year by year.

The Community was right to consider the soup run as of central importance, since it enabled contact to be made with destitute men and allowed an initial appraisal of their attitudes and needs. The men must, of course, make the initial approach but thereafter contacts might become more active. This, above all, was the area in which the volunteer workers needed encouragement and supervision. Because of the naturally informal nature of the work, it was easy to lose the value of any initial contacts made, particularly if the worker concerned did not go out on the soup run again for another week. It seemed sensible to have a soup-run director who could make reports on any promising contacts so that these could be followed up. Volunteers might have tours of duty on the soup run during which they would go out several nights a week. In addition, the idea put forward by the workers themselves, that other activities should be undertaken in order to provide more contacts with destitute men should be systematically considered. The activities of the Industrial Therapy Organization (including car-washing, for example) might also be considered, since it would be extremely useful to foster contacts during the daytime as well as at night.

More attention to the way in which the soup run, and other such activities, could be made to serve the purpose of contacting and resettling the men, would lead to a lower referral rate to the assessment centre, but probably to a more efficient use of the centre and its associated houses. However, a gap would be left which at that time was filled by accepting men for a brief stay of a few days. It was suggested that an extra service be set up to fill this gap.

Another way of getting into firm contact with the men would be to provide shelter for a few days, simply in order to give them a breathing space or a few square meals, without placing them under any obligation to be 'rehabilitated'. This function would best be provided separately from the assessment centre. Experience might well suggest that a lower level shelter might also be provided, analogous to that envisaged by Simon, to which a man could take his bottle if he wished. Alternatively, a series of 'pads' might be provided with no obligations except that St Mungo's workers would have access to them. In this way, men who rarely frequented the soup run might be attracted. Arising out of these contacts, particularly if some continuity of interaction between the men and the workers could be ensured, there might well be opportunities to attract men into the other stream of services. The shelter service would be under the direction of the leader of the soup run.

The assessment centre would, if these recommendations were accepted, become mainly a short-term centre (up to one month) for appraising the men's disabilities and needs and selecting those who could move into the medium-term houses. The leader of the centre should have a professional training and also take overall responsibility for these houses. One of his main functions would be to supervise the work of the group leaders and the volunteers in the houses.

Familiarity and experience of the principles of the therapeutic community would be useful as well as a knowledge of the other social services available. There was no reason why the assessment centre and its surrounding houses should not become a useful addition to the services provided by local authorities and other voluntary agencies in inner London. This would be in line with the recommendations made by Tidmarsh and Wood.

If the selection process were successfully improved, it would be necessary to increase the number of medium-term houses.

One group of three houses was, at that time, already operational, and a group leader had been appointed. It was suggested that two other groups already planned should also be brought into operation as soon as the increased demand from the assessment centre justified it. It would be important for the workers in the houses, and the three group leaders, to retain a close association with the soup run and other basic activities, perhaps through a duty system during which they worked several nights a week on the soup run for a period of several weeks. Experience would tell whether this would be better organized by a system of secondment to the assessment centre during this time or whether they would continue to work in the houses.

The houses should be organized as 'therapeutic communities' and the workers should be encouraged to participate actively at regular meetings of their group of houses, and also at meetings of the staff of all nine houses plus the assessment centre. As the whole system enlarged, the principle of group decision-making would inevitably disappear, but part of the skill of a successful leadership would be to carry the whole group along with it and never to get too far from feelings at the grass roots. Failure to maintain this balance could result in the failure of the whole enterprise.

Long-term houses should be set up as the need for them arose. At the time of the pilot study, there were enough such men in the three medium-term houses to designate one of these houses as long-term. A further medium-term house could then be set up and thus the whole process would be perpetuated. It was difficult to say in June 1972, what the demand for these houses would be, and it seemed unwise to plan for large numbers before experience suggested they would be needed. It was suggested that the basic unit of three medium-term houses would require enough 'permanent' residents to fill one long-term house per year but this estimate might need revision in the light of experience.

The administrative arrangements for the longer-term houses would need to be different; since the accommodation could well be in bed-sitters, fewer staff would be needed and leases would have to be longer-term. Consideration would need to be given to the possibility of the provision of some kind of sheltered work, either through the use of statutory services or by special schemes such as those of ITO. For example, it had earlier been suggested by the Director that a small-holding might be utilized to provide occupation and recreation.

These recommendations, which are paraphrased here from the original report following the pilot phase work, expressed the essence of the research team's view of the way St Mungo's was really operating, as opposed to the image (that of rapidly resettling destitute men) that it had of itself; a view that the Department to some extent shared. It seemed more realistic to attempt to capitalize on the fact that some men, at any rate, stayed long enough to become influenced by the milieu in the houses, and to assume that some of these would only become 'resettled' in the sense that they would live in long-stay sheltered accommodation (though this might include, at best, bed-sitters with minimal supervision). Those who did not stay very long, often remained in touch with the Community, and the institution of a day and night shelter, and the maintenance of contact on the soup run, would provide opportunities for them, too, to come back to the houses from time to time and, eventually, perhaps, to settle.

In summary, the first four recommendations were:

(i) the addition of the goal of settlement in sheltered accommodation to that of rehabilitation to an independent mode of
living

(ii) the provision of a night shelter

(iii) the adoption of a daytime rehabilitation programme together
with a system of daytime contact in order to supplement
contacts made on the soup run

(iv) the appointment of skilled group leaders and a skilled person
to supervise the soup run, in order to guide the work of
enthusiastic but untrained volunteers.

Policy changes in response to the four recommendations

The four recommendations were accepted in principle and implemented in part. A further group of houses was added (group II), and another group that had originally been created to help deal with the men made homeless when Butterwick Rowton House was closed by the local authority, was integrated into the system (group III). The expectation that men would move on was changed and many were encouraged to stay.

The recommendation to provide a night shelter was also adopted, in order to facilitate contact with the many short-stay admissions that could no longer be coped with in the houses. At the end of March 1973, a night shelter catering for fifty men was opened in a disused church (St Anne's) in Westminster. A St Mungo pamphlet explaining its function said that it was intended to provide an unpressurized environment offering 'some security without the threat of institutionalization'. It was hoped that some men would 'acclimatize' and be willing to stay there. By mid-October 1973, there were five workers at the night shelter, together with a variable number of probationary workers. Men were admitted to the shelter, by ticket, after eight o'clock in the evening, and had to leave by seven the following morning (eight on Sundays). Whilst staying at the shelter they were given soup, bread and tea with a breakfast of porridge. In December 1973, this shelter was supplemented by a much larger building, the disused Marmite factory in Vauxhall, capable of housing, at shelter level, 100–200 people. In the Spring of 1975, St Anne's was closed and night shelter provided only in the Marmite building.

One of the prime aims of the night shelter was to increase contact with those destitute men who were not able to accept the relatively more formal atmosphere of a house (permissive though it was in many respects). There would, of course, still be a further group unwilling even to make use of the shelter. It seemed possible, however, that contacts with both groups might be fostered by providing some daytime activity. During the initial period of observation before the pilot study, St Mungo's had carried out 'street cleaning' and provided morning tea for destitute men at the former Covent Garden Market. This had been undertaken as a three-month experiment because local authority cleaners had, on occasion, used water cannon to soak the men sleeping out there, in order to get them to move on, so that the pavements could be cleaned. The workers undertook the cleaning instead, both to protect the men and also because it was an additional means of keeping in contact with them. The scheme was ended (against the wishes of the workers) because the Director felt that it was too much of a strain on staff who were already tired through

having been on the soup run. However, the research team's suggestion of alternative ways of keeping contact during the daytime was
given a great deal of consideration. The campaign known as 'Winter
Survival' began during November 1972, culminating in a three-day
Christmas party at Covent Garden. An ambulance owned by St
Mungo's was used to tour areas of likely daytime contact, in order to
provide medical and welfare help to the men contacted. A further
winter survival campaign was begun in October 1973 but the expense
of these enterprises made their future uncertain and St Mungo's was
unable to continue to afford the running costs of the ambulance. It
was not possible to establish a Day Centre although management and
workers agreed that it would be desirable to do so. Similarly, ideas for
providing some form of remunerative 'sheltered' work were canvassed but could not be put into operation or, like the workshop set up in
Notting Hill in November 1973 for stripping and painting furniture,
proved not to be economically viable.

St Mungo's accepted the part of the fourth recommendation that
concerned skilled group leaders. By 'skills', the research team meant
either relevant professional training, such as social work or probation
work, or long experience in the field of destitution (or, ideally, both).
Shortly after the recommendation was made a St Mungo document
(summer 1972) commented on 'the role of the worker'. After a
description of the 'framework of near equality' existing in houses
between workers and residents it concluded that

> 'whilst attempting to keep the principles of the Community with
> regard to equality firmly in mind, it has nevertheless been essential
> for the continuity and expansion of the project to provide adequate
> salaries to attract certain kinds of workers; especially senior work
> ers, who would wish to spend some considerable period of time in
> the Community.'

The document further stated that three Senior Social Workers and a
Deputy Director were ready to commence work and that an administrator had already been appointed.

Group leaders were eventually appointed to take charge of all the St
Mungo groups of houses. They included qualified people with experience in social work, the probation service, and the rehabilitation of
prisoners. Workers with long experience of the community have also
worked in this capacity. St Mungo's eventually distinguished between three types of staff: part-time voluntary, full-time short-term

(defined as working for periods of six months to a year on board, lodging and pocket money) and full-time long-term. The latter group was salaried. The aim of these distinctions was to build up a substantial core of experienced and qualified staff.

Fifth recommendation: more intensive contacts with residents shortly after discharge

Data from the register set up in October 1972 are given in Part II of this chapter. They indicated that none of the measures so far adopted had resulted in men staying longer in the houses. During the spring of 1974 the research team made a fifth recommendation, that there should be a concentration on readmitted men rather than first admissions and increased contact with men shortly after discharge in order to arrange further admission if they wished this.

St Mungo workers kept in contact with a large number of the men (at least two-thirds) who left the houses, mainly by meeting them on the soup run. Because of the counter-attractions of alternative subcultures, for example in a drinking school, it was suggested that men should be readmitted as soon as possible after leaving, if they wished this. It seemed likely that some workers had tended to give up such men for lost, and had avoided readmitting them.

The recommendation was accepted. Indeed, it reflected a return to an earlier policy. In a St Mungo paper entitled 'Report of first year's work', it was stated that a man met on the soup run, might

'come with us on the rest of the run, and will arrive back at about four or five in the morning. Usually sleeps in a chair and departs at about six or seven in the morning, before most people are awake. He then returns to his former haunts for about a month, then starts again. He then comes and stays until about breakfast and off he goes again and this time he stays until lunch. Again, off for a week, and then his fourth try is usually the important one. He either comes in and stays for a while or does not come again for another few months. (We have found that the person who stays on his first try, never makes much progress. He inevitably shows promise and mixes well, but he cannot seem to stand the strain of total acceptance and thus departs, usually after about ten days.) We have found that this magic figure of fourth time lucky, if the person stays for over eleven days, stands an excellent chance. During his periods of coming and going, he is obviously seeking our motive, he feels it is too good to be true, being a fatalist he is seeking the inevitable catch.'

The emphasis here was on a cumulative effect. St Mungo's had postulated that destitute men, homeless in some cases for many years, would only gradually be induced to 'resettle'. There was no evidence that this was so, since the variables affecting the process were only vaguely defined, imposing difficulties of measurement. Certainly, for many men known to the research team, 'a fourth time lucky' did not occur, but it was possible that the general process postulated might hold true over a sufficiently long period of time. We hoped to quicken this process, if it existed, by a policy of concentrating upon a specific group. This would indicate the extent, if at all, to which such a process was operative.

The recommendation was discussed at a St Mungo Conference held in May 1974, and it was agreed by the staff that it should be implemented. The minutes of the conference stated that

'It was agreed after examination of the various projects that we had a real commitment to the men already known to the Community and energies should be re-directed towards helping them. One way of doing this (bearing in mind that summer was almost upon us with its influx of new people with accommodation problems into London), would be by limiting admissions to . . . (the night shelter) . . . in the main to men already known to the Community and by extending their tickets for longer periods if required, to encourage them to consider house admissions.'

This system stayed in operation and was effective, in the sense that there was indeed a concentration, recorded in the register figures, on men who had previously been admitted to St Mungo's. Unfortunately, however, they did not stay any longer than before (see Part II for figures).

Sixth recommendation: modification of the 'no-drink' rule

Because of the failure of the measures adopted so far the research team decided to undertake a study of the reasons why men left St Mungo houses. Information was obtained about a group of sixty-four men who left during October and November, 1974, nearly half of whom were interviewed. Useful information about the reasons why the others left was collected from case-notes and workers. Eleven men had left mainly because of difficulties with other residents (often one particular man who was found irritating). Such problems were often the result of intolerance of handicap in others. Three residents gave dislike of staff as their reason for leaving. They thought the regime too rigid and censorious. Only one man gave dissatisfaction with amenities as the reason, but two men found the house dull and boring, and two thought there was too high a turnover, with not enough stability. Only one man gave lack of contact with friends outside as his main reason.

It was found that about half the men had left because they were determined to have a drink and could not do so while remaining in St Mungo accommodation, or because they were asked to leave by the staff because it was discovered that they had been drinking. Not all these men were 'problem' drinkers in the sense that their drinking was uncontrolled; about one third seemed to be 'social drinkers' who rarely drank to excess.

'Wilfred', for example, was a 'social drinker' who was asked to leave when he returned to a house after drinking a moderate amount. When asked about his opinion of the 'no-drink' rule he said:

'It is much too strict. If you have half a pint it has the same consequences as being drunk. This total ban on drinking makes relationships difficult. How are you supposed to explain to your friends at work that you can't go to the pub with them because you're not allowed to drink? I wouldn't mind other residents coming into the house if they'd had a drink or two. If they behaved badly, the rest of the residents would be quite capable of dealing with them. If we were allowed this responsibility we'd feel it was more our house.'

Wilfred found the house satisfactory in other respects. It was comfortable and he had had no wish to leave it.

'Brian', by contrast, had a serious alcohol problem and specifically left the house to go drinking. He said:

'I felt that I had to have a drink. I left because I wouldn't break the rule by drinking in a house. I liked everything about the house when I was there. It was magic after what I'd been used to. I really liked one of the house workers. We had known each other a long time on the soup run before I was ever invited back to a house. The other residents in the house were fairly easy to get on with. Drinkers that I knew lived in St Mungo houses a short distance away and we used to visit each other. One used to come here for breakfast sometimes. As far as the drink is concerned it's the total abstinence that creates such strain. I know full well that I need to drink but I can do it in moderation if I have to. I've managed it when I've been working. They don't like you drunk there.'

None of the men interviewed expressed a wish to go back to sleeping rough. Some, especially among the 'social drinker' group, were bitter about the way they had been treated. A minority, at the time of interview, were uncertain whether they wanted anything more to do with St Mungo's. Only one drinker thought that the 'no drink' rule, as it was then applied, was beneficial to residents.

On the basis of these findings the research team recommended that the 'no drink' rule should be relaxed for an experimental period. It was further suggested that St Mungo's should cease to treat drinkers as a homogeneous group and should plan its house facilities accordingly.

Two distinct types of drinker were recognized during the enquiry. One consisted of men with serious alcohol problems who belonged to drinking schools. These schools were closely knit sub-cultures whose members were often bound by strong emotional ties arising out of long periods of association and mutual assistance. A second type was the social drinker. These residents had no problems with alcohol in an addictive sense and could drink or remain dry as they chose. They were often involved, however, in social relationships in which an important activity was communal drinking. It was customary, for example, for some building site workers to go for a pint after finishing work in the evening. It was also common for men working as kitchen porters to have access to alcohol during their working hours. Both occupations employ large numbers of men who have been or are resident in St Mungo's.

The research team suggested that an effort should be made by St Mungo's to attempt a specialization of its service facilities, in order to help more effectively with the various problems of the men admitted to its houses. It was suggested, for example, that a special house or houses should be used by members of drinking schools, with the aim of fostering the close links already existing between them within a more settled and comfortable environment. Social drinkers, likewise, should have their own house or houses. This recommendation was given added weight by the finding that, after infringements of the 'no drink' rule, the most common reason for men leaving the houses was interpersonal differences; to a large extent these were based on a low tolerance of varying kinds of handicap.

Although the research recommendation that special houses should be designated for members of drinking schools and social drinkers was not implemented by St Mungo's (new houses were not acquired and it was thought that large scale movements of residents between existing houses might be unsettling for the men), the relaxation of the 'no drink' rule was accepted as policy for an experimental period beginning on 1 April 1975. This relaxation was still in operation at the end of the research project. The new policy stated that men would only be refused admission to a house, when resident there, if they were actually drunk, or if their behaviour at the time, whether they were drunk or not, seemed likely to upset other residents. Even if a man was drunk, he was free to return to a house as soon as he had sobered up. Drinking *in* the houses, however, was still forbidden. Weekly meetings were to be held at which group leaders, workers, and a member of the research team would be present. These conferences would discuss the reaction of different residents to the new policy. If a resident returned to a house persistently drunk, day after day, or if he persistently annoyed other men staying in the house while under the influence of drink, he would be asked to leave. This decision could not take place, however, until the next meeting was convened and it had to be accepted by a majority of the staff present.

Although the new policy was generally welcomed by workers and men, and seemed to operate well in practice, it did not result in men staying longer than they had stayed before.

Further Changes in the Community

Several events that occurred during 1974 and 1975 should be recorded parenthetically, although they did not result from the recommendations of the research team. The first was the acquisition by St Mungo's, in May 1974, of the old Charing Cross Hospital, which had accommodation for 190 men, mostly in ten dormitories, but with a number of cubicles and single rooms. It was intended primarily for working men but there were exceptions and, theoretically, men in the houses could have been 'resettled' there.

In December 1974, a large bed-sitter complex, called Lennox Buildings, was opened by St Mungo's in Vauxhall. This had about sixty beds, mostly in single rooms. The accommodation was intended for men without severe handicaps, who could look after themselves, since very little supervision was available. Most were referred from agencies other than St Mungo's (e.g. social service departments and reception centres). In a census of residents taken on 1 October 1975, only seven out of fifty-six men were from St Mungo houses.

These innovations did not much affect the situation in the houses although they entailed a rapid growth of the St Mungo complex of services. A decision that did, however, give rise to comment from house workers, was that they should no longer operate the soup run. From April 1975, it was run by 'volunteer' helpers, who were relatively inexperienced and could not get to know the men, both because there was no senior worker equivalent to some of the seasoned workers who had formerly become acquainted with large numbers of men who regularly used the soup run, and because the volunteers did not service the soup run sufficiently regularly or often to build up such experience for themselves. This change was made by St Mungo management and was not in line with the recommendation of the research team concerning the use of experienced staff on the soup run.

Seventh recommendation: assessment of men in the houses

The failure of the research recommendations made on the basis of the attitudes of men leaving the houses resulted in a change of direction in the research. Attention was now directed towards the men who *stayed* in the houses. It was hoped that the characteristics of these residents would provide insights concerning the kind of men most likely to find the houses acceptable. The eventual aim was to utilize this information in an admissions procedure. The research team therefore made a further recommendation that the characteristics of residents staying in houses at least a month should be assessed.

Three separate assessments of men who had stayed as long as a month in two groups of houses were made during 1975, by a member of the research team (JL) in consultation with group leaders and workers. The object was to assess the residents' drinking and social behaviour and derive an appropriate plan of action for each one. Current behaviour in respect of alcohol was classified as non-drinking, social or controlled drinking (an occasional episode of drunkenness was accepted), and uncontrolled drinking; the last being reserved for fairly frequent bouts of drinking usually leading to drunkenness. A few cases on the borderline between the second and third categories were placed into the second but, in general, the distinctions were not difficult to make. Social behaviour was classified according to a hierarchy, with 'aggression' at the top. Only a man who was quite often physically violent or very verbally abusive was regarded as aggressive. A second category of behaviour, not used unless the man was non-aggressive according to the definition, was 'eccentricity', applied only when a man's behaviour was decidedly odd or inexplicable. A man who frequently laughed and talked to himself, or who had very unusual mannerisms, or was extremely suspicious of everyone and everything without apparent reason, would be regarded as showing eccentric behaviour. There was no question of any diagnosis of illness; the observation was purely behavioural. A third category, only used if the other two were absent, was 'withdrawal'. Again, only very marked and active withdrawal was accepted for a positive rating.

Table 4(1) shows the average of three separate assessments of these qualities made in May, August, and November, 1975. In the first place, it can be seen that no markedly aggressive man stayed for longer than a month. This was due to a St Mungo policy of excluding

Table 4(1):   *A classification of the drinking and social behaviour of men who had stayed more than a month in Group I and II houses, May–November 1975 (average of three surveys)*

social behaviour		drinking behaviour			
		no drinking %	contained drinking %	uncontained drinking %	total %
aggression	%	—	—	—	—
eccentricity	%	20.2	7.3	4.6	32.1
withdrawal	%	0.9	5.5	0.9	7.3
none of these	%	11.9	35.8	12.8	60.6
TOTAL	%	33.0	48.6	18.3	—

(average no.=33)

most seriously aggressive men or asking them to leave. A varying, but substantial, proportion was very eccentric in behaviour (some of these men, of course, were also withdrawn). Such men tended to stay longer in the Community than the others. Of the twenty men assessed as markedly eccentric (several were resident on two or more of the census days), nine were known to have been in psychiatric hospitals, and another three had marked psychiatric symptoms at the time of assessment. Severe withdrawal, without accompanying eccentricity, was not common. The largest category, on all three occasions of observation, was that of men who did not show markedly unusual behaviour in any of these respects, although they might well have lesser degrees of eccentricity or withdrawal.

Frequent uncontained drinking was uncommon; there were only six or seven men in the two groups of houses who were often drunk. This shows, however that changing the no-drink rule had had an effect. Quite a large proportion of men took a drink, but without usually getting drunk, and this would previously have led to their being asked to leave.

An estimate of the optimum type of accommodation and need for care was also made on these three occasions, about the same men. The options lay between remaining in a St Mungo house for a short, medium, or long period of time (defined respectively as under six months, six to twelve months, and over one year), transferring to a St Mungo bed-sitter, to Charing Cross, to Lennox Buildings, or to independent accommodation, these alternatives representing pro-gressively lesser degrees of care. The assessments were distributed in much the same fashion on each occasion. The large majority of men were regarded as needing to stay for a long period of time in a St Mungo house. This was particularly true of the eccentric and with-drawn men. Overall, 57 per cent were thought to need long-term care, 18 per cent medium-term, 2 per cent short-term, 16 per cent a St Mungo bed-sitter, and 7 per cent the other types of accommodation. There was little relationship between these accommodation plans and drinking, but non-drinkers tended to stay longer than the other two groups.

In spite of these assessment exercises and the resulting increase in the understanding of the men's behaviour by workers, there was still no evidence that a large number of men were 'settling' in St Mungo houses, although the intake diminished towards the end of the year as more 'unsuitable' people were excluded (see figures in part II).

In order to utilize the experience and information derived from the assessment exercises and apply them directly to the admission process, a routine referral procedure was therefore adopted in November 1975. Men in the Marmite night shelter, which now housed up to 150 people a night, who seemed possibly suitable for one of the houses, were discussed at a weekly meeting at which the Deputy Director, a Marmite worker, the Group I leader, representatives of workers in all three groups of houses, and the research sociologist (JL) were present. An attempt was made, not only to assess whether an individual was likely to settle in St Mungo's, but to consider which house would provide the most congenial atmosphere or company given his behaviour and disposition. Most admissions to houses subsequently came to be made after following this procedure.

Eighth recommendation: routine referral procedure

During the early part of 1976, it appeared that the introduction of a routine assessment procedure before referral might at last begin to have an effect on the numbers settling in the houses, although it was too soon to demonstrate this in the register statistics. An analysis of changes in the house population, together with details of the figures for length of stay, will be found in Part II. Changes in the attitudes and satisfaction of workers will be described in Chapter 5. One further stage in the action research process will be described briefly here, in order to complete the overall picture.

In a report made in January 1976, the research team pointed out that St Mungo's provided two kinds of service; one to men 'on the streets', and the other to men in the houses. (There was also the accommodation provided in the old Charing Cross Hospital but this was more comparable to that in common lodging houses, and was not of immediate relevance to the research.) A basic activity still remained, the soup run, which had still not missed a night since the Community was founded. Its nature had, however, changed. Originally it had been the main method of contacting and interacting with destitute men, getting to know those most likely to be suitable for houses and then, at a suitable moment, bringing them into residence. This was not an effective technique so far as resettlement was concerned, but it was an essential link between soup run and Community. By early 1976, Community workers had little connection with the soup run and the main source of referral to houses lay elsewhere. Moreover, there were many other charitable handouts (though none as regular or unfailing as the St Mungo soup run) so that it was no longer possible to suppose as the workers once had, that the men had no other source of food. It was difficult, however, to imagine St Mungo's without its soup run, which was almost a symbolic activity, and there was no doubt of its humanitarian value.

Some of the functions of the soup run, as a means of selecting men for the houses, had been taken over by the Marmite shelter, where large numbers of men were being accommodated. A substantial proportion of the men were using the shelter regularly and a long-stay group was accumulating. The admission procedure was relatively informal and a division into 'wet' and 'dry' areas ensured that men need not be turned away simply because they were drunk. Some areas were of somewhat higher standard than others, though not up to the standard provided in the houses or in the residents' section of the Camberwell Reception Centre. There were only seven staff, so that it was impossible to develop the kind of caring relationship found in the houses. After the first free night, men were expected to register at a Social Security Office for benefit, and thereafter had to pay for their accommodation. This procedure seemed certain to exclude a number of the more isolated and thus placed St Mungo's a further step away from the soup run clientele.

Most of the daytime activities had proved ephemeral, for lack of staff to initiate and keep them going and, in the case of the Winter Survival campaign, lack of funds to maintain the ambulance. It had not proved possible to start forms of sheltered work. However, it was clear that the provision of food and shelter, on a casual basis, was acceptable to large numbers of destitute men and that, at this level, St Mungo's contributed a useful and substantial supplement to the services of other voluntary and statutory bodies.

The research team felt that the relationship between the 'street' services and the houses had become considerably more tenuous than they had been in the early days of the Community although both type of activity, in themselves, were very useful. At a meeting with management on 15 March 1976, it became apparent that the underlying economics of the situation might well separate the two even further. Clearly, far more men were receiving shelter at Marmite than in the houses, and far more were 'settling', in the sense that they frequently returned to the shelter, although their basic style of life was not really changing. Marmite could help hundreds of men, while the houses could only help tens. Moreover, the houses were far more expensive to run, even though the leases were relatively cheap, because of the numbers of workers.

Various plans were being considered by management: one option was to concentrate on shelter services entirely, to set up a welfare centre in a temporary building near a site where men slept out so that they could easily obtain the price of a night's shelter, and to discontinue the soup run. Another was to amalgamate several of the houses, so that fewer workers would look after more men, in order to decrease the cost. This would mean, as the research team pointed out, a dilution of the caring relationship, and a consequent difficulty in looking after the more handicapped men. Management were less convinced of the importance of this relationship and suggested that St Mungo's should not try to provide a service for the handicapped, since this was a matter for the statutory services. Cogent arguments can be made for both points of view (see discussion in Chapter 7).

The position of the research team in this debate was that the development of both types of service had been logical, indeed it was going according to plan, although more slowly and with more fluctuations than had been hoped for, and that the potential for them to continue in close interaction with each other remained, and should be exploited. This would mean, in particular, utilizing to the full the energy and experience of the workers (on the soup run, at the shelter, and in the houses), coordinating with the statutory medical and social services, and looking for extra sources of funding in order to be able to set up more houses and supervised bed-sitters. Many men were now staying in the houses for a year or more and could be settled in 'group homes', thus making more places available in the houses. The flow of men from soup run to shelter to a stable residential environment would thus be maintained. This would be a rational development in the light of earlier studies, such as the one at Camberwell, and a continuation of the strategy worked out on the basis of the pilot phase of research.

Summary

Following the pilot stage of research, it was already apparent that any expectation of the immediate resettlement of a substantial proportion of men, with the characteristics described earlier, was unrealistic.

Two more specific aims were therefore suggested. One was the provision of relief and shelter, of the same kinds as those provided by many other voluntary organizations, but more systematically organized, and deliberately used to further the second aim. This was to attempt to help a larger proportion of men to stay in the houses, on the assumption that this would either help towards their eventual resettlement or would, in itself, constitute a worthwhile outcome. These were the fundamental conclusions, reinforced by all the subsequent work, and the recommendations made during the action research followed logically from them.

The strengthening of the soup run and the provision of night and day shelters, and other daytime activities, were recommended to help the men 'on the streets', and it was not thought that such humane activities needed justification by research. The appointment of a trained group leader to supervise the soup run and others to be in charge of houses, with the use of house workers on the soup run and other 'street activities', were designed to foster the interaction between these front-line services and the houses, so that more men could be induced to settle in the latter. A whole series of recommendations, based on small research studies, was made in order to foster this latter aim: an increase in the number of houses to permit some to be designated long-term; the provision of bed-sitters; trained group leaders; a concentration on readmitted men and on men who were known to the Community; the involvement of house workers in the assessment of individual men and the formulation of a personal plan of help for each one; and the institution of a routine assessment procedure for all men admitted.

The effect of these recommendations and the subsequent changes in policy will be considered in Part II.

Part II   Effectiveness of St Mungo services

Criteria of effectiveness

The evaluation of an organization that claims to have a service function should be made in terms of the extent to which it reduces or minimizes social disablement and therefore social need (see Chapter 1, p. 16). In the case of the St Mungo Community, whose object was to help men who regularly slept rough to find and maintain their own accommodation*, the definition of need appears relatively simple. It will be agreed that a man needs a roof over his head, a regular means of subsistence, and some of the comforts of life ordinarily enjoyed by other people in his society. When the man has been sleeping in a doorway or on a park bench, and subsisting on the proceeds of begging and charitable 'hand outs', it is fairly easy to measure progress. The main problem for evaluative research, therefore, is to determine whether a reduction in need, if any can be demonstrated, is actually due to the 'treatment' received. No doubt some of the destitute men contacted by the St Mungo Community would have made progress anyway; others might have made use of different services, such as reception centres or other hostels. A further problem for the evaluator concerns the extent of need; how many destitute men contacted by the St Mungo Community on the soup run were not accepted into one of the houses and how many men did not even make contact with the soup run? Finally, there is the question of the methods whereby any success in the resettlement of destitute men is achieved – are there techniques specific to the St Mungo Community that could with advantage be used elsewhere?

The most basic question for the research team concerned effectiveness in reducing need, since if none could be demonstrated, the question of whether the reduction was greater than that achieved by other agencies and, if so, how it was achieved, would not arise at all. Two kinds of standard were employed by the research team for assessing the effectiveness of the St Mungo services. One was the expectation, fostered in the early literature of the St Mungo Community, that its methods were successful in resettling destitute men in their own accommodation. In order to evaluate this claim a series of follow-up enquiries was undertaken by the research team, throughout the lifetime of the project, in order to discover what happened to residents who left the houses. Only if the rate of resettlement of these men in their own accommodation was, or became, fairly high, would it be worth considering an elaborate evaluative design, including appropriate controls.

The second kind of standard used for assessing the effectiveness of the St Mungo services was more modest than the first. This was the extent to which destitute men became settled in St Mungo houses.

*See page 53 for a definition of 'own' or 'independent' accommodation.

Given the fact that the men using the St Mungo services did not 'progress' to the extent of finding independent accommodation, and given the fact that many of these men had been sleeping rough fairly regularly with only occasional brief periods in the accommodation provided by voluntary and statutory agencies for destitute men, any degree of settlement within St Mungo houses could, in itself, be regarded as a measure of success. The subsequent progress of the men, whether in 'long-term' houses, St Mungo bed-sitters, or in more independent accommodation, would provide a further index of effectiveness.

Follow-up

In order to assess the extent to which residents were resettled in independent accommodation a regular check on the whereabouts of men who had stayed in St Mungo houses was made every two months, by a member of the research team who had known many of these men when a worker in the St Mungo Community, and who had been the most experienced worker on the soup run (SP). Information about the men's whereabouts was gathered from the statistical register, from workers, from London reception centres and from voluntary organizations.

The most influential follow-up study was carried out during the first few months of 1972 as part of the pilot phase. The thirty-five men in residence in the four DHSS-funded houses (Group I), comprising an assessment house and three hostels, on 1 January 1972, and the twenty-nine men admitted during February, formed the sample. A check on the whereabouts of these sixty-four men was made during the first week in May. Only eight were untraced, and these were thought (on the basis of the outcome of previous admissions) to have returned to their former way of life. *Table 4(2)* shows the details. It is doubtful whether more than three men, at most, could be said to have changed from a completely rootless way of life, characterized by lengthy periods sleeping rough or frequent accommodation in lodging houses or reception centres, to something more settled, as a result of spending several months in St Mungo houses. In nearly all cases, the pattern after leaving St Mungo's was much the same as the pattern before admission. The main characteristic of the houses was a rapid turnover, with two-thirds of the men admitted being back on the streets within a week. Only about 15 per cent stayed for three months

Table 4(2):   *Follow-up status in May 1972 of 64 men in Group I houses in January and February 1972*

status in May 1972	resident on 1 January 1972 (N35)	admitted during February (N29)	total (N64)
own room	4	1	5
with relatives	1	2	3
with friends	1	–	1
Part III accommodation	1	–	1
lodging house	–	1	1
St Mungo house	19	8	27
prison	3	2	5
living rough	4	9	13
not traced	2	6	8

or more. On the other hand, St Mungo workers did retain contact with a large proportion through the soup run.

Similar follow-up enquiries were repeated many times during the course of the research project and the results were always very similar. For example, a regular check on the whereabouts of men who were resident in St Mungo houses on 1 October 1972 was made every two months, utilizing information from the statistical register and the workers. There was very little change in the mode of life followed by these men during the subsequent four years. In April 1976, twenty-four out of fifty-six men could not be traced (eighteen of whom had disappeared almost at once after a very brief stay in the houses). Of the rest, twenty-five were in accommodation provided by the St Mungo Community (nearly all in the houses of Groups I, II, and III), one was in contact on the soup run, one was in hospital, two were in Part III accommodation, and one had died. Only two men were living in their own accommodation.

Another group of 114 men, admitted to St Mungo houses between 1 October 1972 and 28 February 1973, was followed up, in the same manner, at two-monthly intervals until April 1976. A large proportion of this group could not be traced at all (N62), leaving fifty-two men whose whereabouts were known. Of these, twenty-three men (including nine in the Marmite night shelter, and one in Lennox Buildings) were living in St Mungo accommodation or had recently been in one of the houses. Seven men were in reception centres, three in hospital, and three in prison. Eleven were squatting or sleeping rough and one had died. This left only two men in their own accommodation, and two in lodging houses, who might be said to have changed their former mode of life.

Other follow-up enquiries were undertaken, throughout the lifetime of the project, showing what happened to various groups of men whose whereabouts were known after they left St Mungo houses. None of these enquiries allowed a more optimistic assessment of outcome. It has been suggested that the shortest-term follow up is the most complete, and also, perhaps, provides the best test of the efficacy of any method of rehabilitation (Wing 1966). The follow-up enquiries carried out during the pilot survey, therefore, probably provided as good an index as any of the efficacy of the St Mungo experience in leading to an independent settlement. Only eight out of sixty-four men followed-up in the pilot survey were untraced and these had stayed only a very few days in the houses. Forty-six of the remaining fifty-six men had made no progress at all. Even out of the remaining ten, only three could be said to have benefited from a lengthy exposure to the St Mungo regime. This rate of success (5 per cent) was hardly large enough to make controlled studies necessary. Follow-up enquiries into the whereabouts of groups of men admitted to houses in later years did not show an improvement on this rate of resettlement.

Length of stay in St Mungo Houses

Because of the St Mungo Community's lack of success in the resettlement of destitute men in independent accommodation the focus of interest shifted to the number of men who could be induced to settle in the St Mungo houses. The criterion of 'settlement' used was that a resident should remain in a house for at least three months. This, of course, was an arbitrary period and it was not expected that residents' attitudes and motivation would greatly change during this time. A measure of some kind was necessary, however, and it seemed reasonable to suppose that a three month stay in a small (and, in many respects, 'homelike') hostel would mark a change in the life style of many of the men. Clearly, however, the pattern of 'resettlement' would have to be considered in assessing the effectiveness of the St Mungo services. If most men remained in a house for little more than three months and then returned to the destitution 'circuit', an assessment of 'success' would need to take this into account. In fact, as will be apparent, this was not the case.

The methods used to bring about an increase in the numbers of men settling in the houses were described earlier in the chapter. Here, we shall be concerned only with the results of the policies followed by the St Mungo Community, as monitored by the statistical register. Figures could be given for monthly or even weekly occupation of the houses. They would not, however, give much more information than the summary tables included here.

Table 4(3) shows the number of men resident in the night shelters and houses on eight six-monthly census dates from October 1972 to April 1976. The expansion of the organization is evident. The numbers of men in houses nearly doubled by October 1973 and thereafter remained fairly constant. The proportion of places occupied in houses varied, but was usually 75–80 per cent.

Table 4(3):   *Number of men resident in shelters and houses on six-monthly census dates*

| | *shelters* | | *houses* | | |
	Marmite	*St Anne's*	*available beds*	*occupied beds*	*occupancy %*
(31 Dec 1971)*	—	(7)	(—)	(28)	(—)
1 Oct 1972†	—	8	66	42	64
7 Apr 1973	—	20	98	72	73
6 Oct 1973	—	54	116	84	72
6 Apr 1974	207	56	120	99	83
5 Oct 1974	closed	30	126	95	75
5 Apr 1975	76	19	115	91	79
4 Oct 1975	132	closed	101	83	82
3 Apr 1976	108	closed	104	84	81

* The night shelter at St Anne's had not yet opened.
† The register started on 1 October 1972.

Table 4(4) shows the numbers of men admitted to houses during three consecutive one-year periods, and a final six-month period, from the time when the statistical register was started in October 1972. The admissions are divided into 'first-ever' (men who had never been in a St Mungo house before) and re-admissions during the period. Since each man might be admitted several times, the total

Table 4(4):   *Number of admissions to houses and proportion staying 3 months or more*

	number of men				
	first ever admission	*not first admission*	*number of admissions*	*staying 3 months +*	
				N	*%*
October 1972–September 1973	154	103	413	64	15.5
October 1973–September 1974	172	150	483	80	16.5
October 1974–September 1975	83	135	362	65	18.0
October 1975–March 1976	39	28	75	38	50.7

number of admissions during the period is also given. Finally, the table gives the number and proportion of admissions that resulted in a stay of at least three months.

During the year October 1972–September 1973, there were 413 admissions to the houses, sixty-four of which resulted in a three-month stay (15.5 per cent). Of the 257 men admitted, 154 (60 per cent) had not been in a house before. Thus, there was a considerable turn-over of men staying in the houses without very much success in the way of resettlement following. The number of house places available was increasing during this period, and the St Anne's night shelter catered for many of the 'short-stay' men (see *Table 4(3)*). During the following year, out of 483 admissions to the houses, eighty, or 16.5 per cent, resulted in a three-month stay. During this period the Marmite night shelter was opened for a few months, the St Anne's night shelter continued to operate, and a few more places in the houses were made available. Since the numbers of men staying three months or more in the houses were not increasing very much, the research team suggested a concentration on men already known to the St Mungo Community (see page 64). Of the 322 men admitted during the year, 172 (53 per cent) had not used the houses before, a proportion not very much lower than the previous year. During the third year, October 1974–September 1975, the measures adopted to facilitate a concentration on the group of men already known to the St Mungo Community began to have a certain effect, in that the numbers of 'first-admitted' men (most of whom were now admitted to the Marmite night shelter) began to decrease. Only eighty-three out of 218 men (38 per cent) had not used St Mungo houses before. The total number of admissions also went down, although the number of places available in the houses remained much the same. There was, however, very little evidence that more men were settling in the houses. The proportion of men staying in houses at least three months increased slightly to 18.0 per cent but the actual number of 'longer-stay' men went down compared with the previous year (from eighty to sixty-five). During the final six-month period, October 1975–March 1976, the new referral procedure for men staying at the Marmite night shelter was put into operation (see page 69) and this resulted in a sharp reduction in the number of men admitted to the houses. (The figures shown for this period in *Table 4(4)* should be doubled in order to make them comparable with a full year.) On the other hand a much larger proportion of men (50.7 per cent) stayed for more than three months in the houses, and the numbers involved suggested that the referral procedure was beginning to have an effect.

Table 4(5) shows the length of stay of men in the houses on successive census days, beginning with 1 October 1973 when the number of places available had approximately reached a plateau. The figures show that the number and proportion of men who had been resident in the houses for more than three months increased markedly after October 1975 (39=46.4%; 55=59.1%; 43=55.1%; 64=76.2%; 70=94.6%). During the last few months of the research project very few men were admitted to the houses, since the places there were already occupied. It was apparent to the research team that unless many of the 'longer-stay' residents (at the last census, forty-four out of seventy-four men had been resident in the houses for a year or more) could be regarded as being permanently settled, and other houses opened to accommodate the men staying at the Marmite night shelter, the movement of men from the night shelter to houses would come to a halt altogether.

Table 4(5):   *Length of stay in St Mungo Houses*

	0–3 months	4–6 months	7–9 months	10–12 months	over one year	total
1 October 1973	45	6	13	5	15	84
1 October 1974	38	9	12	6	28	93
1 October 1975	35	5	1	6	31	78
1 April 1976	20	18	11	5	30	84
13 August 1976	4	11	11	4	44	74

Reasons for the increased length of stay

Two factors seemed to operate to produce the increased success of the St Mungo services in settling men in the houses. The first was the new referral procedure, the second the fact that the selection of men for houses was made from a night shelter, rather than (as had previously been the case) the soup run. The assessment of the needs of men prior to house admission had become much more thorough than in previous years. The men's problems and the ability of the St Mungo Community to help them were considered, and particular care was taken to ensure that men were placed into an environment that seemed likely to be congenial to them. To this end the likely reaction of men to the residents and workers in particular houses was discussed.

The information necessary to make this procedure work was available because men were able to stay at the night shelter. The shelter attracted large numbers of men. Admission on the first night was free, entrants were not required to undergo a selection procedure, and the premises were so extensive (accommodating nearly 200 men) that men probably felt confident of getting a place and so were motivated to visit the night shelter regularly. Because men went there regularly (some every night) it was possible for shelter staff to maintain contact with them over a long period. In this way contacts were initiated with many of the more withdrawn men. The night shelter, with full-time staff, allowed more continuity of contact than the soup run. The needs of the men were now considered more systematically, whether they chose to ask for house admission or not. In these ways, the St Mungo selection process came to resemble that followed at a reception centre, when men are selected for the residents' section.

Several criteria were used in selecting men for admission to the houses from the night shelter. Men were usually required to have stayed in the shelter for a period of at least three or four weeks. Some men who only used the night shelter very infrequently, did so when their usual accommodation was unavailable (for example, when a Salvation Army hostel was booked-up). The workers wanted to exclude such men from the houses on the grounds that their need for accommodation was less than that of men who slept at the night shelter regularly and who otherwise usually slept rough.

In selecting men for houses, the night shelter staff tended to choose those who appeared very isolated. Some men would stay at the shelter night after night without talking to anyone unless approached by one of the staff. It seemed likely that men who were withdrawn in this way would find it difficult to get help, since this would often depend upon their making the first approach to an agency. Other men were offered a house place because they were currently experiencing a crisis which was felt to require help within a more settled environment. Thus, some men suffering from a mental illness, who displayed symptoms at the night shelter, were approached regarding house admission. In cases of this kind the ruling regarding length of stay at the shelter was waived.

Once the system of referral became operative the houses rapidly filled. In mid-August 1976, of seventy-four residents, seventy (95 per cent) had stayed for three months or longer in the houses, and forty-four of these had been resident for a year or more. What recommendations could be made concerning the development of the St Mungo Community (and, more generally, for the provision of services for destitute men) depended on the extent of the need of these men for sheltered residential accommodation and other services. In order to assess this the research team interviewed the residents. The next section is devoted to the characteristics of the men then accumulating in the houses.

The characteristics of men in St Mungo houses in April 1976

The research team interviewed all but two of the sixty-one men who had been resident in the houses for three months or more on 30 April 1976 (in many cases these men had been interviewed before and were well-known to the research team). Only two residents could not be interviewed. One refused, and the other, living in a St Mungo bedsitter, could not be contacted in spite of repeated efforts, so that this, too, was probably a form of refusal. The schedule of questions used to guide the interview was an abridged form of the one used in the survey of April 1973, three years earlier, when thirty men who had stayed longer than three months in St Mungo houses were inter-viewed (see p. 52).

Table 4(6) summarizes the results from the April 1973 and April 1976 resident surveys. It was evident that the men accumulating in the houses in April 1976 gave at least the same history of destitution and other problems, such as psychiatric hospital admission, prison sentences, and excessive drinking, as did those interviewed three years earlier. Tidmarsh and Wood found that the men at the Camberwell Reception Centre were, on the whole, truthful in the details they gave about their earlier experience, although a check on prison sentences and psychiatric hospital admission did increase the proportions somewhat. No check of this kind was undertaken in the St Mungo surveys since the research team did not consider that the

Table 4(6): *Characteristics and attitudes of men newly admitted to St Mungo houses compared with those remaining three months or more: April 1973 and April 1976*

	admitted 1.10.1972– 28.2.1973 (N67) %	resident 3 months+ 1 April 1973 (N30) %	30 April 1976 (N59) %
age: 51 +	48*	71	59
birthplace: England or Wales	34*	77	37
length of stay: over one year	NA	13	53
marital status: single	63	70	53
often slept rough	54	33	68
ever in psychiatric hospital	25	20	53
ever in prison	50	46	39
in prison 5 times or more	28	15	42
ever problem with alcohol	39	15	7
			27
asked for suggestions by staff	13*	38	12
talks to staff often	76	76	49
staff appear friendly	83	93	86
other residents have similar problems	30*	61	46
satisfied with food	94	72	56
satisfied with sleeping accommodation	86	87	81
satisfied with day accommodation	88	77	NA
satisfied with recreation	62	73	NA
satisfied with homeliness	73	70	58
want to stay as long as possible	78	64	56
prefer accommodation in digs	10	17	29
unlikely to become independent	67	59	64

* Difference between first two columns significant beyond 5% level (Chi-squared)

value of the extra information justified getting informed consent from the men. The figures shown in *Table 4(6)* are therefore minimal. If anything, the 1976 group of residents had been even more disadvantaged than the 1973 one, and the fact that larger numbers of men had been induced to remain in the St Mungo houses did not at all seem to be due to selection of men with fewer handicaps. One fifth of the 1976 residents had first slept rough twenty years or more previously, and nearly as many had spent at least a year sleeping rough continuously, without using any other form of accommodation at all. More than half (56 per cent) of these residents had not worked at all during the year prior to their last house admission. Higher proportions of residents in 1976 than in 1973 said they came from Scotland or Ireland and the age of the men was considerably younger. Twice as many as before said they had been in a psychiatric hospital and nearly twice as many said they had had a problem with alcohol.

It was apparent from the interviews that many of the men now settling in the houses had additional problems as well as a need for accommodation. The prevalence of psychiatric disability was particularly prominent. The proportion of residents staying in houses at least three months who said that they had been in psychiatric hospitals doubled between April 1973 and April 1976 (from 20 per cent to 39 per cent). This was due in part to the experience gained by workers in undertaking, with the research team, the assessments of residents' needs (see page 53). The assessments often resulted in the development of contacts with local health and social services in order to make specialist help available to the men. In one group of houses, for example, a community psychiatric nurse was assigned by the local hospital to advise the workers and to act as a liaison between the houses and the hospital. Once links of this kind had been established it became apparent that many men with symptoms of mental illness, who previously had been rootless for long periods, began to settle in the houses. This outcome resulted in some men with similar problems being referred to houses from the night shelter. At the time of interview nearly one-fifth of the residents were attending psychiatric out-patient clinics. In many cases, the alternative to the small St Mungo houses, with their high degree of staff support and close links with professional services, was undoubtedly a brief stay in hospital followed by a return to a circuit of unsuitable lodging houses or rooms, with spells of sleeping rough between.

The assessment exercise carried out in 1975 in the house of Groups

I and II (see *Table 4(1)*, p. 70) was continued during 1976 and a final assessment was made on 13 May 1976. A classification of the drinking and social behaviour of the forty-four men who had stayed a month or longer in the two groups of houses on that date showed very little change from the earlier assessments. Once again, no men with markedly aggressive behaviour were present and most of the men showed no really severe social abnormalities though a substantial proportion (nearly a third) could be regarded as markedly eccentric in behaviour.

A plan of further care, made by house-workers and the social scientist (JL) for each of the forty-four men, indicated that most were likely to require supportive care for some time. Two were thought to need 'medium-term' care (6–12 months) and twenty-six 'long-term' care (a year or more). It was thought that thirteen would be able to live reasonably well in partially-supervised bed-sitter accommodation, while the other three could manage without supervision in subsidised housing.

Part III   Men with psychiatric disorders

In view of the prevalence of psychiatric disorders among the men in St Mungo houses, it was decided to make a detailed study of one of the three groups (Group III) in order to describe the problems presented by residents and the methods used by workers to cope with them. In the event only two of the three houses in the selected group could be included, because of a management-worker dispute at the third (see Chapter 5). However, these two houses were characteristic of St Mungo houses as a whole at that time.

There were nineteen residents and four workers in the two houses. Of the nineteen residents, nine had disorders that house workers thought might be psychiatric. The other ten were middle-aged or elderly and had been destitute for long periods before coming to St Mungo's. Several were in poor physical health: two had heart disease (both died during 1977 while still resident), one had a chronic chest complaint and one severe arthritis. Another man, aged seventy-nine, was confined to his room by a multitude of infirmities.

The nine with possible psychiatric disorders were interviewed by a psychiatrist (JW) during December 1975 and January 1976. Brief notes about their past histories, present state, and the problems presented to house workers, will be found in the Appendix. Three had schizophrenia, two had severe memory deficits (one due to traumatic brain injury, one due to Korsakov's psychosis), two had been severely depressed (one had various physical disabilities, the other was moderately mentally retarded), two were chronically incontinent of urine (one of whom was severely handicapped because of either schizophrenia or pre-senile dementia).

Only one of these men (Mr Lambert) could fairly easily have been accommodated elsewhere. He illustrated the problems described by Hewett, Ryan, and Wing (1975) in their study of psychiatrically disabled clients financially supported in voluntary and statutory hostels by three London boroughs. It was all Mr Lambert could do to maintain himself in an unskilled packing job. He came back exhausted in the evenings and contributed nothing to the running of the house. He would have been quite unable to look after himself. Because he tended not to take oral medication, he needed regular fluphenazine injections to suppress active symptoms of schizophrenia, but suffered from side-effects (parkinsonism and overweight). He was one of the few men in St Mungo's who had never actually slept on the streets (though he had lived for years in a cheap lodging house). He was also the only man in the two houses still in touch with a relative (his elderly mother lived nearby). The community psychiatric nurse gave helpful advice to house workers concerning his management.

The two men with memory defects presented special problems to the house workers, who had to rehearse their itinerary with them before they went out, provide them with a list of streets, shops and other items, and make sure they had a card with their address on it in case, as often happened, they got lost.

The two incontinent men had frequently been turned out of accommodation because of their disability. One was clearly deteriorating and it was only a matter of time before he would have to be admitted to hospital. The other had found a sheltered niche which suited him very well, and he made as little trouble for house workers as his condition allowed.

The other two men had multiple problems. They could perhaps have lived elsewhere but only in accommodation which provided the same degree of shelter and support, since they tended to become severely depressed when on their own.

The house workers were, in effect, acting as housekeepers and unobtrusive supervisors. They undertook the shopping, the management of the budget, the cooking, and much of the cleaning. The staff-resident ratio was relatively high and the salaries of some of the workers not much lower than that of equivalent staff employed by local authorities. It is possible that a few of the men could have lived under less sheltered conditions, for example in group homes, but this would not have been feasible for most. If all the St Mungo houses had had good medical and nursing support, both from psychiatric hospitals and from general practitioners, and good social support from the local authority, they would have formed part of the varied and flexible support system which is essential if 'community care' is to work.

None of the men was local, in the sense that he 'belonged' to the area. Mr Lambert's mother lived nearby, but he himself came from elsewhere. The concept of 'community' had very little meaning for most of the men. They were passively solitary and, in most cases, had been so all their lives. The original idea that small permissive units would gradually enable them to recover a lost interest in other people was proved wrong. Long and devoted efforts to draw them out did not succeed. To sit with them in the houses was mostly to sit in silence; efforts at conversation lapsed for lack of response. The house workers used naturally occurring situations such as mealtimes and domestic chores to foster contact but they rarely managed to stimulate spontaneous communication. Without spontaneity on both sides (not just from staff, however much status boundaries are consciously blurred by them), no attempt to create a community can be said to have succeeded. By contrast, however, the atmosphere of the St Mungo night-shelter was impersonal and institutional. The degree of supervision and care, the standard of living, and the opportunities for interpersonal contact, were incomparably better in the houses, even though to the average householder, they would have seemed rather decrepit, dirty, and uncomfortable.

Summary

We have described, in this chapter, the long process of action research whereby a modest aim of settlement in St Mungo houses was substituted for the original goal of rehabilitation towards independent living, and a series of proposals were put forward by the research team (many of them accepted by management), which eventually led to the modified aim being realized. The successful technique was based, first, on the self-selection of men making regular use of the night shelter and, second, on an assessment of these regular attenders and the offer of a place in the house thought to be most suitable for selected individuals.

Other techniques, such as more intensive contacting of men after discharge, relaxing the 'no drink' rule, appointing more experienced group leaders, and attempting to create a 'therapeutic' atmosphere in the houses, had little effect. Once the selective process was instituted at the night shelter, the houses filled very quickly.

The men accumulating in the houses at the end of the research project were mostly severely disabled and there was little likelihood that many would be able to achieve independent status. It is probable that they had not been selected earlier, partly because of a reluctance on the part of management to accept handicapped people (who, it was thought, should be the responsibility of statutory services), partly because the men did not put themselves forward and did not catch the attention of St Mungo workers, either on the soup run or at the night shelter.

Thus St Mungo's had set up a useful chain of services leading from the streets (the soup run), through the night shelter (with 'wet' and 'dry' areas), to supervised houses and bed-sitters. This created the opportunity for some men to move one or more steps up the ladder, and even to progress from the streets to relatively independent accommodation. Unfortunately, such movement could only occur if there was a constant provision of extra places in the upper tiers. Since funds were not available for providing more hostels or bed-sitters, the available accommodation rapidly filled and management decided to concentrate resources at the level where most men could be accommodated, i.e. the night shelter. This had to be done at the price of a lower quality of life and an abandonment of movement 'up the ladder'.

This lack of resources had also been evident earlier in the project when it proved impossible to set up or maintain a range of daytime activities in order to extend the contact between workers and men. It proved impossible for a voluntary organization to do more than plug gaps. The changed response, both ideological and practical, of workers and management to these necessities will be described in Chapter 5, before a consideration, in Chapter 6, of new developments in the statutory services.

Appendix   Brief portraits of some of the men who stayed in St Mungo houses

These brief vignettes are included in order to illustrate some of the problems that destitute men pose to helping agencies, problems which the men have been unable to cope with by themselves. The first man, Mr Adams, is representative of a considerable number with a long-standing history of social failure who used St Mungo houses, particularly in the early days. Most such people tended to move on quite quickly but Mr Adams stayed for a year and seemed to derive much support and help from the Community. The second man, Mr Barnard, also stayed several months but the amount of attention given him did not result in any change in his way of life. The third man, Mr Chandler, provides a good example of the kind of practical assistance that can be given by helping agencies.

The other nine men were living in two St Mungo houses at the time of the survey in January 1976 described in Part III of this chapter. They are characteristic of the sort of men who accumulated in the houses towards the end of the period of action research and clearly illustrate the way that St Mungo's was filling in gaps in the health and social services.

In all twelve cases, personal details have been disguised.

Mr Adams, aged 21

This young man was with the community for one year. He was brought up in Scotland. Nothing is known of his parents save that they neglected him as a child and as a result he was shunted at various times to an aunt and a grandmother. After leaving school at fourteen he ran wild and became involved in gangs of youths in the town. According to his own account he became very aggressive and had a number of short prison sentences. How disturbed he really was is difficult to determine because one of his characteristics was to create an aura of notoriety about himself in order to attract attention from the residents and workers. He joined the army but, not liking the discipline, he bought himself out after seven months and came to London where he hoped to 'join the scene'. He worked in an illegal strip club for a few months and when the police raided the club, he was sentenced to three months in jail. When he came out of prison he lived in Salvation Army and Rowton houses or slept rough. When he dislocated his arm, he asked to come into the Community.

He was a tall, lanky, bushy-haired Scot with an aggressive manner and broad accent. In the Community his insecurity became very apparent. He needed to know everything that was going on and if he heard a new piece of information, he would pretend to have known it all along. This tendency together with low intelligence made him very easily led. Often in an argument he would become dogmatic and aggressive if he felt that he was losing, and it was very difficult to ask him to do anything without his becoming hostile. When he spontaneously began anything himself, he would resent any interference, saying 'I'm in charge'. He occasionally stole things and once brought back seven pairs of tights. Everything he said had to be taken with a pinch of salt. His planning ability and foresight was very limited and he could not manage money. For example, he bought a tape-recorder, leaving himself no money to pay the rent. He had no friends. Although he liked girls, he became giggly and immature in their presence, showing off and trying to impress. He worked quite regularly during the latter part of his stay in the Community as a ward orderly in a teaching hospital, helping occasionally in the house. After staying for a year he found himself a good room nearby and left.

Mr Barnard, aged 47

Mr Barnard was one of the most aggressive individuals that the community tried to help. He was a thin, hollow-cheeked man, always needing a shave. He came from London, an illegitimate infant brought up in an orphanage until he was fourteen. He had no family connections and no friends. 'Bad company' as he called it, and the absence of any trade, led him into a life of petty crime for which he had received some twenty-six convictions. He often drank heavily and was occasionally addicted to barbiturates. In 1941 he entered the army and apparently enjoyed his period of service. He left in 1948 and was subsequently admitted to at least five psychiatric hospitals. He was tense, highly strung, and subject to depressive moods, occasionally of suicidal intensity. He was often aggressive, once having spent seven years in prison for 'grievous bodily harm'. In the last job, with an electrical firm, he allowed a length of cable to be stolen while he was away at lunch and was put on a three-year probation order. The probation officer referred him to the community for support and rehabilitation.

In St Mungo's his behaviour continued to be disturbed. He collected articles from all over the community in his room. He would blankly deny any responsibility, offering no explanation for the presence of the missing objects in his room. Persisting argument would lead to an aggressive outburst, the occurrence of which he would later deny completely, appearing 'all sweetness and light.' At other times he would remain in a thunderous mood, picking quarrels with residents and workers alike. Threats to kill two of the residents were expressed with sufficient force to create a few days of heightened tension in an already charged atmosphere. Threats to kill himself or take all the pills in his possession were not uncommon and he would lock himself in his room in order to produce the maximum of consternation. He had a large collection of pornography, much of which was devoted to whipping and lesbian practices. He settled a little when he found work in a bakery, but he was discovered stealing again, charged, and sent to prison for a further three months.

Mr Chandler, aged 74

Mr Chandler came from the North of England, one of a family of five, his father being a labourer. After leaving school, he was called into the army and saw active service during the 1914–18 war as a private. He began labouring after the war and continued this all his working life. He was seldom out of work, moving about the country. He never married and had few friends, preferring his own company. He had never been in any serious trouble and eventually he became a respectable old age pensioner ending up in Part III accommodation. The institution was large and was gradually being closed down. He had to find other accommodation and, being an independent person, preferred to walk out and live on the streets. However, he found living rough extremely difficult, and gradually became physically unwell. At this point he was found by the community. He was almost unable to walk when met. He was a white-haired, stooped man, taking ages to dress, after which he would go to the local betting shop. He never seemed to win anything. The rest of his pension he spent on tobacco and a newspaper which he always read thoroughly. He was a popular figure in the house. Pressure on the local authority obtained a place in

Part III accommodation where he went very willingly as the atmosphere was good and the house contained only sixty residents.

Mr Davies, aged 61

Mr Davies had run away to sea at the age of sixteen, and eventually became a bosun in the Merchant Navy. He was married and had three children. Eleven years earlier, he had been knocked down by a lorry when drunk, and had suffered a subdural haematoma. An operation to relieve this was unsuccessful and he was left with a damaged brain. Thereafter, he alienated all his family and friends and lost touch with them. He could not work or manage money, and wandered from hostel to hostel, often living rough for long periods. He had been in contact with St Mungo's via the soup run for five years and had previously spent short periods in St Mungo houses.

At interview, he spoke rapidly but often incoherently about his past life, dwelling in excessive and repetitive detail on various scenes, e.g. trying to recall every word of a conversation, and then losing the thread. He often used words wrongly: e.g. 'My wife's name was a German', meaning that his wife was a German. He was unable to remember the names of his children or of the house workers, and did not know the date, month, or year. He was quite unable to do simple arithmetic. He helped with chores around the house and was quite satisfied to be there. He did not want to be in hospital. The house workers managed his pocket money, always checked where he was going when he went out, and made sure that he had a card with the address on it, in case he got lost. Otherwise, he needed little supervision. He would not have been able to care for himself, and seemed well-placed where he was.

Mr Edwards, aged 68

Mr Edwards was a solitary man who had spent his life at unskilled work in the hotel trade, usually living-in. He had always tended to drink too much when he had the money, and he blamed his present situation on this. He had often been incontinent when drunk. According to the case-notes, he had drifted to living in Rowton Houses as he got older, and was finally refused admission because of incontinence at night. For the past ten years he had lived rough, with occasional brief stays in Camberwell Reception Centre and various other temporary shelters including the St Mungo night shelter. He had had to leave St Mungo houses on several occasions because he was drunk. On the present occasion he had been in the house for more than two years.

At interview, he was well-oriented and, though reticent, able to give a good account of himself. He was incontinent of urine every night and had been so for more than ten years. Investigations had all proved negative. He refused to wear a portable urinal. He tended to drink when depressed, but rarely now had enough money to get drunk. He had various ailments: 'heart trouble' (probably intermittent cardiac asthma), a pronounced limp (possibly a congenital dislocation of the left hip), and arthritis of the fingers of both hands. He was quite contented where he was, but thought the Reception Centre had suited him best. The house workers said he washed his own sheets every day, shared a room with Mr Gerrard (also incontinent, see below), and presented little problem in the house. He always kept entirely to himself. It seemed doubtful whether any other placement would be as suitable.

Mr Frost, aged 65

Mr Frost had always been solitary. He had lost a leg in an accident when a young man but had usually been able to find work in the hotel industry until his late fifties. He had been known to St Mungo's for seven years, often sleeping on the embankment and taking soup there. He had been in houses several times for brief periods but had been in the present house for four years. Occasionally he had had temporary work, e.g. as a night-watchman. Recently, he had had a heart attack, and thereafter his activity had been restricted and he became depressed.

At interview, Mr Frost was moderately depressed, but said his mood was improving. He had always liked being active, and the heart attack had stopped his long walks (he managed his artificial leg very well). Recently he had been able to go out again, and felt better for this. He did not know the whereabouts of his relatives, could not get on very easily with other residents, and found very little pleasure in life. The house workers said that he was out all day, helped with the chores in the evening, and enjoyed a conversation with them, although he kept aloof from other residents. He seemed to have settled in the house, but might perhaps be better placed in Part III accommodation. He did not want to be in hospital.

In October 1977, Mr Frost was asked to leave the house by the senior workers of the group because of non-payment of rent. He was advised to go to the St Mungo night shelter. He was found dead the following morning on Shepherds Bush Green. The cause of death was heart failure.

Mr Gerrard, aged 49

Very little was known about Mr Gerrard. He had first contacted St Mungo's over four years earlier, on the soup run. Everything had to be repeated several times before he understood it, and his own speech was confused. He mumbled to himself. He had come to the house eighteen months earlier from the night shelter. He was completely isolated, eating by himself in the kitchen. He never kept himself clean without prompting, and reminders irritated him. If asked to help with the cleaning, he slopped water about in a messy way, and generally made everything dirtier. The part of the room which he shared with Mr Edwards was, as the house worker put it, 'meticulously filthy'. He was incontinent every night, but never admitted the fact and his sheets had to be washed for him. He spent long periods in bed, and sometimes shouted to himself. It was difficult to imagine any other setting that would have tolerated him for so long, and it seemed inevitable that he would eventually have to be transferred to a hospital under order.

Mr Gerrard did not speak at interview. His condition was compatible with pre-senile dementia or severe schizophrenic deficit.

Mr Howells, aged 55

Mr Howells was an unmarried Irishman, who had never had any schooling. He had spent his life as a labourer in the building trade, usually living in common lodging houses. He drank heavily when he had sufficient funds. He had suffered from pulmonary tuberculosis but recovered. Three years earlier he had been in psychiatric hospitals several times, after serious suicidal attempts, usually discharging himself after a few days. It was thought on one occasion that he had been psychotically depressed. He had always been solitary, and found it difficult to talk to others, partly because of a stammer. In recent years he had often slept rough and had lived in derelict houses. He had been in the house for more than a year, and had settled down well. He spent his days walking the streets, coming back at about 6 pm. He helped about the house with very simple tasks but kept to himself and often would not eat with the others. He had an irritating habit of humming loudly to himself.

At interview, he was very reticent (his usual manner), and it was not possible to assess his intellectual level, though it seemed likely that he was moderately retarded intellectually. He seemed well-placed in the house.

Mr Ingram, aged 59

Mr Ingram was a Scotsman who had been brought up in an orphanage, and had lived a solitary, friendless life, finding casual work as a kitchen porter. He had always drunk heavily when in funds and also gambled a great deal. He had been sleeping rough for at least thirteen years, mostly in London. He had been in psychiatric hospitals on at least four occasions, and the last time had been given antabuse to help control his drinking. He had complained of auditory hallucinations, which were not solely related to drinking bouts, and was diagnosed as suffering from schizophrenia. The community psychiatric nurse administered an injection of fluphenazine once a fortnight. He said he had had three operations for duodenal ulcer and frequently complained of various aches and pains – headaches, stomach pains, etc. He first contacted St Mungo's via the soup run and had been in the house for four years. He did not help with chores, and spent much of his time in bed.

At interview, he had a variety of complaints, which he had said had been present for years, and which he attributed to a germ picked up from a potato machine. Among these were pains in his calves on walking. He had to stop every 100 yards or so (probably thromboangitis obliterans). He also described hearing voices almost continuously; mostly his relatives talking about him. Sometimes the voices would start in the rumblings of his stomach. He thought the wireless was brain-washing him. He had drunk at least ten pints of beer a day for years, when he had been able to afford it, but now rarely drank more than a pint. He was quite content where he was and thought the injections helped to muffle the voices. He did not want to return to hospital and seemed well-placed.

Mr Jenkins, aged 53

Mr Jenkins was a Londoner, who had been in the Army for five years and had then been a street trader. He married on leaving the Army, but his wife left him after a few years. There were no children. He was never licensed as a street trader and was frequently prosecuted. He also worked sporadically as a kitchen porter and had long periods of unemployment. For seven years he had lived in derelict houses, his only companion being a dog. He had been admitted to psychiatric hospitals on several occasions and thoroughly investigated because of a history of venereal disease without positive result. He said he could hear noises and voices in his head, thought he was Julius Caesar and a champion runner, and that his legs were worth millions of pounds. (He had been known to other street traders as 'the poor millionaire'.) He talked to himself and said that he was two people. The final diagnosis was schizophrenia. He had first contacted St Mungo's three years earlier, and had been in the house for about a year. He still had his dog, and spent most of his time walking the streets. When helping with chores (which he did rarely), he had a habit of doing everything three times, e.g. washing up a cup three times before drying it. He was taking phenothiazine medication orally and was under the care of the local psychiatric hospital. His former wife still visited him occasionally.

At interview, he was very remote in manner, and answered questions with only a few words. He was well-oriented and denied hallucinations. He had no plans for the future, and was content to stay where he was. He did not want to return to hospital, and seemed well-placed.

Mr King, aged 55

Mr King was an Irishman, who had been a stoker in the Merchant Navy until 1968. He was a good worker, but drank increasingly heavily. His wife left him because of this, and they had no children. He had been living rough for many years and had several times been admitted to psychiatric hospitals where the diagnosis was Korsakov's psychosis and cirrhosis of the liver with oesophageal varices. On one occasion, he had delirium tremens. He had been referred to St Mungo's after leaving prison (where he had been sent for vagrancy) and was given a bed-sitter. However, he was quite unable to cope on his own and was referred to the house two years earlier. He kept to himself, feeling superior to other residents, and spent most of the time out walking. He had one job as a night-watchman but was sacked for forgetting to close the gates.

At interview, he was pleasant in manner, and talked readily. The chief problem was his poor memory. He had no idea of the date, month, or year, could not name the street the house was in, and said that he could not rely on remembering any piece of information he needed, although sometimes his memory seemed to be quite good. He could subtract sevens rapidly and accurately, and named correctly several people he had known in hospital, but he could not recall a four-figure number. He thought he might be able to work as a hotel porter, but this seemed very unlikely. He was philosophical about his disability and did not get depressed or worried by it. He still drank when he could, but his money was rationed by the house workers. He seemed well-placed where he was.

Mr Lambert, aged 47

Mr Lambert had been in the Navy for eight years, and had then become a trolley-bus driver for six years. He married when he was eighteen. When his daughter was fifteen, she was remanded on a charge of shoplifting and then committed suicide. Mr Lambert was admitted to a psychiatric hospital soon afterwards, and thereafter had three more admissions, altogether spending several years as an in-patient. He showed characteristic symptoms of schizophrenia during acute attacks. During this time, his wife divorced him, and thereafter, he lived in lodging houses. Recently, he had been in a 'doss-house', and had neglected himself a great deal.

At the time of his last discharge, sixteen months earlier, he was referred by the local hospital to St Mungo's, and had been living in the house ever since. He found work almost at once, but lost the job after a few months because he was too slow and kept poor time. Three months before the interview he had found another job, as a packer, and so far had kept it. He received an injection of fluphenazine every three weeks from the community psychiatric nurse. Occasionally he became rather depressed and took to his bed, but most of the time he was quiet and pleasant though very withdrawn. His mother lived nearby and he visited her regularly.

At interview, after returning from work, Mr Lambert described his work (doing up parcels), which he said he could cope with, though he found it exhausting. He denied active symptoms of schizophrenia. His face was expressionless, his posture rigid, and his movements ponderous and slow. He weighed sixteen stone. He had a marked right-sided parkinsonian tremor as a result of a recent injection. He said he got 'depressed in the lower part of his back'. His manner was friendly enough but completely lacking in spontaneity. He only answered direct and simple questions. He was content with the house and did not see where else he could go.

5 A community in transition

The early development of the St Mungo Community

It is not surprising that some reactions to the problems posed by persisting destitution have been impatient and radical. One such response, as we have seen, was the Simon Community. The founder, Anton Wallich-Clifford, was surprised, according to Tully,

'that so many young people accepted this challenge to contract out of square society for terms of 6 months to 2 years. These young workers volunteered with zeal, vision and a desire to contribute to the social reconstruction of the world in which they lived. With an infinite capacity to tolerate, love, tend and integrate, many Worker-Simons built themselves a reputation for taking on an unenviable task and performing it without counting the cost. They served where few had dared to look, let alone live. They were accepted, loved, and respected in return by those who previously felt they could never relate to anyone.'

The small groups of 12–20 people

'existed primarily for those who would never find a place in society, those who needed long-term care. The Simon Community did not have as an aim the rehabilitation of its members. Simon worked with soup runs and shelters at the lowest levels on skid-row. Slowly it assimilated an individual or group into a reception shelter or house of hospitality. The philosophy was to seek social readjustment from within, rather than imposition from above of arbitrary standards. There was a great degree of permissiveness compared with other organizations, because the creation of a free community group was the goal. This permissiveness appalled some critics, e.g. at the first tier level shelter for methylated spirit drinkers, men were allowed to bring in their bottle to the ground floor' (Tully 1970).

Tully went on to describe the 'bitter in-fighting' that developed when different Simon Communities began to adopt different principles, some of them moving towards more traditional aspects of social work. 'Most were disillusioned with the ideals but felt they had not been given a chance.' Finally, due in part to financial difficulties, the Simon soup run and night shelter were discontinued.

It was noted in Chapter 1 that the St Mungo Community grew out of the break-up of the Simon Community and shared many of its early ideals. The young St Mungo workers were motivated by an ideal of service, by the feeling that communal life in small groups of equals was better than most modes of living favoured by contemporary society and perhaps by a romanticism which was proof against the more sordid aspects of destitution. This motivation sometimes proved, however, to be sharply at odds with the general trend of administrative development within the organization, whose management often appeared, to the workers, to be authoritarian and rigid. This is probably the main explanation of the fact that sporadic and, in some cases, bitter conflict has characterized the history of the St Mungo Community.

Before describing the fluctuating relations between St Mungo workers and management it is useful to discuss briefly some general considerations relating to the bureaucratization of organizations and staff conflict. These provide a context for the ideological struggles that occurred in the St Mungo Community during the research period.

Bureaucratic and charismatic leadership

Weber pointed out that bureaucratic organizations have distinctive characteristics. The activities of members are defined in hierarchical fashion with superior officers supervising those lower in the order. Authority inheres in the office rather than in the individual who performs the official role and value is attached to continuity, impersonality, and expert control.

Many voluntary organizations are founded by a charismatic leader who, as Weber suggested, is obeyed by virtue of personal trust in him and his exemplary qualities. Charismatic authority, however, is incompatible with routine administration. If a charismatic leader is successful in publicizing the cause of an organization, and in attracting support for its work, he will create conditions that necessitate a change in the nature of its leadership. As the organization increases in size it will come to require an ordered, formalized system of leadership and administration in order to coordinate its increasing number of activities. A system of this kind is incompatible with the informal, personal, and intrinsically erratic nature of charismatic authority. In consequence, an expansion in the organization's activities will lead either to a change in the 'style' of its leadership or to the replacement of its leader by one whose qualities are considered more suitable for current needs.

The expansion of the organization, and the changing character of its leadership, have far-reaching consequences for its members. Michels (1966) suggested that, as an organization increases in size, there is a need for authority to be delegated, since collective decision-making becomes increasingly difficult. The 'face-to-face' contacts between all members, that Katz (1964) described as characteristic of newly founded voluntary organizations, are no longer possible. The tendency towards delegation is increased by the organization's growing need (because of its increasingly complex operations) for specialized staff.

These developments mean that fewer people can take part in decision-making. There is a tendency towards oligarchy, often associated with a decline in the ideological zeal of the leadership. Blau (1964), in attempting to explain this development, had employed Festinger's theory of 'cognitive dissonance' (Festinger 1957). He suggests that since the members of small, newly-formed organizations might derive little material or status rewards from their work, doubts are likely to beset them about whether the rewards of membership are worth the costs. The 'cognitive dissonance' that results from this situation is reduced by inflating the value of the rewards (a feeling of working towards just and virtuous goals) and depreciating the size of the costs. The importance of ideological principles is therefore emphasized. The members of an 'established' voluntary organiza-tion, however, do not incur similar costs for their activities. Since they are unlikely to experience 'cognitive dissonance' they feel less need to extol the virtues of an ideology and are less inclined to accept charismatic leadership.

The leadership role in a bureaucracy exerts a moderating influence on ideological convictions. This role, in a large organization, is usually one of compromise. Etzioni (1970) has suggested that a leader has the task of coordinating the work of the groups that make up the organization. Each group might have different and partially incom-patible goals. Leaders are also required to accept compromises if they wish their organization to enter into agreements with others. Lipset (1960) discussing this process in trade unions in the United States, has described how the managements of industrial firms sometimes stipulate, in return for recognizing the legitimacy of trade union activities, the need for 'responsible' union leadership. Similarly, a charity funded by a government department will be required to accept conditions in return for this financial support.

These changes in the style and views of the leadership often give rise to conflict among the organization's members. This occurs between the 'idealists', who hold the original principles of the organ-ization to be sacrosanct, and the 'realists', whose ideological views are less intense and who favour some dilution of these principles on the ground that, in the long run, this will strengthen the organization and enable it to achieve many of its aims. The differing sets of values held by these two groups have been termed 'particularistic' and 'univer-salistic' (Blau 1964). 'Particularistic' values are those that distinguish the organization from all others. They will have been the motivating force behind its foundation. 'Universalistic' values are more general-ized and are agreed upon by most members of the community. To help the poor is a 'universalistic' value. The specific measures advo-cated by different groups to achieve this end would reflect their 'particularistic' views.

The bureaucratization of the organization is accompanied by a change in the kinds of value emphasized by the leadership. Increas-ingly, 'universalistic' rather than 'particularistic' values are emphas-ized. This occurs because the leadership is anxious to broaden the appeal of the organization in order to establish and maintain a high level of recruitment and financial contributions.

The decline in the ideological fervour of the leadership will be criticized by those members who believe that a more moderate position betrays the unique, 'particularistic' belief upon which the organization was founded. The leadership, however, will be willing to abandon radical ideals (they might, of course, suggest that this will only be a temporary expedient until circumstances are more favourable) if, as they believe, such advocacy threatens the acceptance of the organization by the wider community and hence its continuing existence.

The emphasis of the leadership on the need for such 'acceptance' is often associated with an excessive preoccupation with means. Merton (1968) has termed this process 'the displacement of goals'. The leadership comes to view the organization as an immediate value rather than an instrument; it becomes an end in itself. The rigidity in policy which can result from this process will be attacked by those members who joined the organization because it seemed to offer a radical alternative to other agencies which they saw as bureaucratic. The leadership, and the professional staff appointed by it, are now seen by many members as possessing the characteristics of Merton's 'bureaucratic virtuoso', 'who never forgets a single rule binding his action and hence is unable to assist many of his clients'. The recognition that 'professionalism' of this kind is present provides, according to Katz (1964), a major cause of conflict.

The evolution of the St Mungo Community

All these processes can be seen in the evolution of the St Mungo Community during the six years (1971–7) of the research project. The expansion of the organization was accompanied by the growth of a formal administrative structure and a diminution of collective decision-making. The number of office staff was increased and an 'Administrator' appointed to supervise the day-to-day running of the organization. These staff were solely concerned with administration, worked in separate offices and lived in private accommodation. They met workers infrequently and residents hardly at all. In order to better coordinate the workers' activities, 'Group Leaders' were appointed by the management.

These developments were sharply at odds with the ideals and motivation of the workers. They believed communal life in small, informal groups of equals to be better than most modes favoured by

contemporary society. So far as they were concerned their commitment, interest, and energy *were* the St Mungo Community and they
considered senior workers, like the Director, to be no more than
experienced versions of themselves. They saw no need for, and were
opposed to, the growth of bureaucratic structures within the organization. Many were critical of the management's decision to accept
funding from the Department of Health and Social Security, fearing
that compromising conditions would accompany the agreement. The
management, however, had decided that the grant was necessary and
felt that some compromise of ideals was inevitable if the organization
was to receive wide support. Without such support, they suggested,
they would not be able to help so many destitute men. The workers,
while agreeing that it was desirable to help as many men as possible,
felt that the management's concept of 'help' (stressing 'quantity'
rather than 'quality') was becoming divorced from their own.

The management-worker conflicts that occurred during the
research period were separated by intervals of relative calm. A period
of mounting tension between the two groups would result in a crisis
which would then be resolved. After a resolution had been effected
(usually by resignations but on occasion by dismissals), the organization would experience a period of quiet. Forces encouraging conflict
were still active, however, and tension would again begin to increase,
the outcome being a recurrence of crisis.

Tension between management and workers was apparent to the
research team during their first contacts with the organization in
1971. At that time, as noted above, many workers were suspicious of
the new relationship with DHSS. Some management statements did
little to allay these suspicions. At one of the St Mungo staff meetings
(29 March 1972) for example, the minutes of the meeting stated that
the Director,

> 'stressed that because of the need for the Community to maintain
> its grants and thereby insure its existence, beds in houses must be
> filled now. Workers were instructed to report to the Administrator
> when a resident left without paying. Also never give rent back to a
> resident. Workers were reminded of the importance of their roles
> and the Community's task within the framework of DHSS. The
> importance of records and filling of bed spaces was paramount.'

Many workers feared that such a policy would erode the principles on
which the St Mungo Community had been founded. One of the

conflicts between the management and the workers that arose at this time illustrates the nature of the differences between the two groups.

The conflict concerned a three-month street-cleaning experiment (referred to in Chapter 4), undertaken by the workers because local authority cleaners had used water cannon to soak men sleeping out in the Covent Garden Market in order to move them on. The workers undertook to take responsibility for cleaning one particular area in order to make this behaviour unnecessary. They also welcomed the street cleaning as an additional means of contact with destitute men. The Director felt, however, that such work was an extra strain on already tired workers and finally decided that street cleaning should be ended, in spite of the protests of the workers. This was a clear-cut directive and the workers had the option of accepting it or resigning. The Director, discussing his decision, suggested that internal dissension arising out of conflicts over such matters detracted from the efficiency of the St Mungo Community. Many workers, on the other hand, felt that the main reason they had joined the organization was that its structure was informal and offered them the opportunity to participate in decision-making, so utilizing their intimate knowledge of the feelings and needs of destitute men.

Another example, cited by workers to the research team, of the increasing divergence between their views and those of the management, concerned the case of 'Ron', a resident who had been drinking excessively for over twenty years before first entering the St Mungo Community. He was not sleeping rough, since he shared a single room with three alcoholic men, at the Angel in North London, but he appeared at the soup run with some regularity, about once a fortnight, when he had been drinking heavily and had no means of transport home. On Easter Monday, 1972, 'Ron' was 'dry' because he had no money. He met a worker on the soup run, and they discussed the chances of helping him with his drinking problem. 'Ron' was very depressed and told the worker that, living with his room-mates, he would never be able to stop drinking. Two weeks later he was seen again on the soup run, drunk, and complaining that he was ill. Because he had been drinking he could not be taken back that night to a house but arrangements were made by the workers to meet him two days later. He was admitted into the St Mungo Community as arranged but disappeared from the assessment house the following morning. Two days later he was readmitted, and four days after that he was transferred to a house in Notting Hill, where he settled in very well. 'Ron' was a quiet man who tended to be reticent and was sensitive about being a 'burden' upon others. He found the house in Notting Hill congenial and was happy there. Three weeks after he was admitted to this house, the leader of Group I moved 'Ron' to another house on the grounds that he was ready for a move to a 'higher-level' hostel and that it was important that he should not become too dependent on the St Mungo Community, since he would eventually have to leave it. 'Ron', according to some workers, did not understand the reason for the move, since he had only recently settled in, and other residents, who had been in his house longer than he had, had not been asked to transfer. Some workers criticized the transfer, arguing that there was no real difference between the two houses and that it was misguided to think that a person with 'Ron's background could adapt to a new style of life in a matter of a few weeks.

In reply to this criticism, the leader of Group I commented that

'Ron was moved to a new house because he was becoming too cosy and was shelving his problem, which would appear to be excessive drinking. The move was intended to help him face up to his problem. When he is too secure his problem does not go away, it just lies dormant. It is anticipated that Ron will break down and eventually have to be readmitted to the Community and will become gradually more capable of facing his problems.'

The leader of Group I also thought that the criticism of his actions made by some workers was misguided since, not being in daily contact with all the houses, they 'cannot see the overall group picture'. He also thought that there could be too much discussion between the workers and other St Mungo staff. 'Limited discussion is fine but it reaches a point which is no longer useful.'

The nature of decision-making within the organization increasingly led to dissatisfaction among workers. This was expressed by one worker who felt that whatever he said at staff meetings was 'just disregarded'. Another worker suggested that the management 'don't run the Community for the benefit of the dossers but so that they can say to the DHSS, "look we've filled so many beds" '. A third worker, discussing the staff meetings, commented that,

'they used to be about residents. The workers pooled their knowledge of the residents and this gave a clearer picture of the people in our houses. Now that's all finished. The emphasis now isn't on people but on trivial things. How can you get to know somebody when your time is taken up with forms and housework?'

Many workers began to regard the Director and the management as increasingly remote from the problems of the residents in the houses.

The Director, commenting on these criticisms, said that he hoped that the decentralization of the organization into semi-autonomous groups (by this he meant the formation of groups of houses) would assist the workers to alleviate their feeling of frustration in the matter of decision-making. The director believed that in a smaller group the 'shyer' workers would feel more ready to participate in discussions and felt that the alienation felt by many workers was a 'symptom more of the personal inadequacies of individual workers, in the face of the enormity of the homelessness problem, than a reflection of any malaise in the Community'. The Director believed that in time he would be able to attract a 'more mature' type of worker.

It seems useful, in a discussion of this situation, to consider how far the St Mungo Community at that time, had the characteristics of a 'therapeutic institution' (the management view of St Mungo's) or of a 'total institution' (many workers believed that the organization was developing in this direction). One characteristic of a 'therapeutic institution' would be a freeing of communications between junior staff, residents, and management. In such a situation, senior staff would know what was happening and what everyone felt about it while junior staff and residents would be aware of policy and able to express their views with some hope of influencing events. A 'therapeutic institution' would also be characterized by an analysis of events in terms of personal interactions and motivations. Other characteristics would be a flattening of the authority pyramid, role-examination, and Community meetings.

Although the St Mungo Community had never formally been a 'therapeutic community', in the sense that it had consciously adopted these principles, it had claimed, in its early publications, to aim at most of them and it would have been possible for the management to make a deliberate attempt to obtain professional staff who had some experience of implementing such a regime. The research team had the impression that there was some retreat under the pressure of rapid changes. The St Mungo Community had not, however, become a 'total institution', though some of Goffman's criteria were satisfied to some extent. Entry to the St Mungo Community was contingent on men attending the soup run, giving up their right to drink, and having their social security benefits collected for them by workers so that their rent could be deducted before they received the residue. However, residents could sometimes opt out of almost every other rule, to the extent that some led rather isolated lives, in spite of being in a small community. The staff-inmate split in the organization was certainly nothing like that found in some other institutions (Goffman 1961; Townsend 1962). The workers were resident, ate with the residents, and shared the same facilities. They took part in all the same household chores and their pay was no better than that of the residents. Nevertheless, the workers' dress was a kind of uniform, recognisably different from the clothing worn by residents and usually comprising jeans, coloured shirts or smocks and beads when they were fashionable. The workers were never called 'residents' and they had the power to enforce the non-drinking rule and thus to exclude the residents from the houses.

However, within the St Mungo Community, the dehumanizing process, considered by Goffman to be characteristic of some American mental hospitals, was certainly not obvious. The resident did not lose in humanity by being admitted to a house and was not regimented or treated as an object. He was free to come and go as he pleased. A privilege system operated in the houses, in the sense that those residents who were most helpful and conforming to the workers were most likely to advance to more comfortable circumstances but this seemed, in some respects, a useful technique and an index of progress. On the whole, therefore, it could be said that the St Mungo Community did provide a non-stressful and non-pressurizing environment, without many actively harmful aspects, although many of the positive aspects of a therapeutic community and of planned rehabilitation were absent from the houses.

The dangers of increasing bureaucracy and central direction in the organization were emphasized by the research team after the pilot survey and we pointed out that such changes needed to be introduced with sensitivity and a regard for the principle of active participation in small groups, which was thought by us to motivate the workers. The alternative might be, the research team suggested, that the seeds of conflict already present within the organization would germinate. The ultimate outcome, if the St Mungo Community survived these conflicts, might then be that it would develop into just another supplier of substandard temporary accommodation for homeless men, run along authoritarian lines and indistinguishable from other agencies already operating in the field.

The second phase of research (July 1972–December 1973)

The debate and conflict that had been evident among the St Mungo staff during the first few years of the organization's development continued and increased during the second phase of the research. The most concrete evidence of this conflict was the resignation of ten workers following a St Mungo conference held at the end of October 1972. These workers felt that the management had paid no attention to their point of view and therefore saw no prospect of the St Mungo Community developing in ways that they thought desirable.

During this period, the research team interviewed two groups of workers: those who had worked in the St Mungo Community for at least three months on 1 October 1972 (N16), and those who had worked there for at least three months on 1 April 1973 (N29). The 'October group' of workers was more pessimistic and disillusioned than the 'April group'. They described low participation in decision-making, excessive discrimination between members of staff and residents, and poor staff morale throughout the organization. The 'October group' preferred a relaxation of the 'no-drink' rule and wanted more participation in decision-making (e.g. in the way houses were run) on the part of residents. In general, the 'April group' was considerably older. These workers were much less critical of the St Mungo Community, described a higher staff morale and did not favour a relaxation of the 'no-drink' rule or more power for the residents. By April 1973 most of the more radical 'longer-stay' workers had resigned.

Twelve of the twenty-one workers who left the St Mungo Community between October 1972 and March 1973 were interviewed by the research team. Eight left within a month of the St Mungo conference mentioned above. None of these workers disagreed with what they took to be the fundamental aims of the organization. Their criticism was that the policies being pursued by the management seemed unlikely to achieve these aims. In particular, there was a strong feeling that decisions concerning the St Mungo Community were made arbitrarily by the Director and management and without prior discussion. Some workers felt that they put in long hours of work, without much advice or help from the management, and were then blamed for infringements of rules that they had not known existed and which, they felt, had sometimes been made up on the spur of the moment. Several workers complained of an arbitrary element in the allocation of work, for example being transferred from one house to another without explanation, and even felt that they were liable to arbitrary dismissal by the Director. Another complaint was that 'emotional involvement' with the residents, which was an inevitable stage through which new workers passed and which many felt to be valuable, was not regarded at its 'true value', being rejected and sometimes derided by members of the management.

One worker made a more general point, suggesting that the enlargement of the St Mungo Community had made a more authoritarian approach on the part of management inevitable, since it had become impossible to discuss the more important issues within the whole organization before arriving at decisions. A more institutional approach had, therefore, to be adopted. Other workers suggested that the group leaders had come to take on some of the attributes of the Director and had begun to regard themselves as a class apart from the other workers; they had also become remote from the residents.

In many cases, these workers had personal reasons for leaving the organization as well as the kinds of reaction mentioned above. These reasons were sometimes closely allied to feelings of disillusion, as in the case of one exhausted worker who felt 'mentally wasted'. In other cases, a need for more personal time, more privacy, more contact with relatives or friends outside the St Mungo Community, added to the problems encountered by the workers within the organization itself. In general, then, this group of staff members was highly critical of the way the St Mungo Community was being run. They had not found in the organization what they had expected nor had they felt that they could influence it to move in the direction they favoured.

The organization seemed to recover from this period of conflict (since many of the most critical workers chose to resign rather than continue working with the management), and throughout much of the third phase of research (January 1974–March 1976), the relations between management and workers were relatively harmonious. Developments were occurring, however, that were to result in a renewal of conflict.

The third phase of research (January 1974–March 1976)

The third phase of research was one of relatively quiet development within the St Mungo Community, as the Marmite night shelter, the former Charing Cross Hospital, and Lennox Buildings were taken over and adapted for use by the management, and as the assessment of the suitability of men at the night shelter for a place in one of the three groups of houses became routine. Most of the dissident workers of October 1972 had left the organization and the history of the episode was known to fewer and fewer staff. However, the management decision that the soup run should be serviced only by volunteer 'helpers' introduced a source of potential conflict to the organization.

As was shown in Chapter 4, the new referral procedure (of men staying in the Marmite night shelter to the houses), together with the evolution of a new group of experienced workers, was to have the eventual effect of inducing more residents to stay in the houses, many of them quite severely handicapped. Because of the severity of the handicaps suffered by these men (see Appendix to Chapter 4), the workers began to develop a caring relationship with the residents which was less ideologically based than that characteristic of earlier phases of the St Mungo Community. Some came to believe (through frequent contacts with health and social services) that 'professionals' such as psychiatrists could help rather than simply 'label' the men, and that some demarcation of roles and authority between workers, group leaders and management might (to the extent that it facilitated a more efficient liaison with outside agencies) result in a better programme of care for the residents. This development did not, however, lead to an improvement in the relationship between management and workers since many workers believed that the administration (however it might be viewed in principle) was, in practice, inefficient.

In order to reassess the relationship between these two groups the research team carried out a further series of staff interviews. By March 1976, there were seventeen workers looking after sixty-seven residents in ten small houses organized in three groups. By contrast, the Marmite night shelter accommodated up to 150 men, served by seven workers. As described in Chapter 4, the two aspects of the St Mungo services (those 'on the streets' and those in the houses) had tended to become separated. Workers in the houses no longer serviced the soup run and the only contact between the night shelter and the houses was the weekly referral meeting initiated by the research team.

The attitudes of St Mungo staff in March 1976

The research team interviewed thirty-five St Mungo staff during
March 1976. All seventeen house workers (twelve of whom had been
employed for three months or more) were included and all seven
workers at the Marmite night shelter (five of these had been employed
for more than three months). In addition, eleven management staff
were interviewed, including the Director, the Group leaders, the
Administrator, and those concerned with accounting, computing,
and personnel management. Most of the secretarial staff, who had
little to do with the residents or the workers, were not included.

The following account is concerned with the twenty-eight members
of staff (80 per cent of the thirty-five staff who were interviewed) who
had been employed for three months or more. These data can be
compared with those of surveys of St Mungo staff in October 1972 and
April 1973. Some of the results are given in *Table 5(1)*. In age and sex
composition the most recent group of workers was closer to that of
1972 than that of 1973; i.e. the 1976 group of workers was younger and
more likely to be female. Few workers, in 1976, expected to stay as
long as two years in the St Mungo Community, compared with April
1973. The educational standard reached by the workers was similar
in all three surveys; most had achieved O-levels or better. Some, in
1976, had relevant professional training.

The outstanding characteristic of the staff interviewed in March
1976, was their low morale. Only 29 per cent of the staff gave a rating
of six or more (on a nine-point scale of personal morale), compared

Table 5(1):   *Some characteristics and attitudes of members of staff who had been
working in the St Mungo Community for three months or more*

	October 1972 %	April 1973 %	March 1976 %
age: 31+	19	41	20
sex: female	50	31	43
length of stay: 2 years or more	—	10	17
likely length of stay: 2 years or more	6	48	23
education: O-level or better	93	73	85
own morale: high	44	79	29
others' morale: high	20	65	11

with 79 per cent in April 1973, and 44 per cent in October 1972. The
rating, by individual staff members, of the general staff morale within
the St Mungo Community, was even lower. This marked decline in
morale was not due to any disagreement with what staff took to be the
fundamental aims of the organization; 63 per cent of staff were in
general agreement, and a further 17 per cent, although they had
mixed feelings, were basically in agreement with these aims. This
finding was similar to those of the two earlier surveys.

The issues of contention expressed by workers in 1976 were much
the same as those expressed in October 1972, but the 1976 group of
workers, although sharing the same motivation as the 'October
group', were much more likely to be salaried and to have 'professional' attitudes towards their clients. In interpreting the figures and
illustrative comments that follow, it should be remembered that the
group of thirty-five staff interviewed in 1976 was not homogenous. In
general, house workers were strongly opposed to certain management
practices, while night shelter workers were divided in their views, and
management and administrative staff were relatively content. For
example, when asked how far the St Mungo Community was self-
governing, 34 per cent of all staff said that there was no self-government
at all, and another 57 per cent said that it was very limited. Among house
workers, the proportion saying 'not at all' was 53 per cent; but among
management and administrative staff the proportion was only 18 per
cent. The point is made effectively in *Table 5(2)*, which shows the

Table 5(2): *Responses by three groups of St Mungo staff to a question concerning the
extent to which the views of workers expressed at a Staff meeting would be taken into
account by those in charge of policy*

% considering views taken into account:	house workers (N17)	night shelter workers (N7)	management and admin. staff (N11)	all staff (N35)
not at all	29	—	—	14
only to a very limited degree	65	71	36	57
to some extent	16	29	37	20
would be seriously considered	—	—	27	9

(All workers included, irrespective of length of stay)

responses of the three groups of staff to a question about whether they thought the views of the workers, expressed at a St Mungo meeting, would be seriously taken into account by those in charge of policy. No further comment is necessary.

Many workers expressed themselves forcibly on the subject of their own powerlessness. They did not believe that the management would be at all interested in their views. On the few occasions they had mentioned these, most said they had either been ignored by the Director or actually shouted down. No fewer than fourteen out of seventeen workers said that the Director would not be at all interested in their views on running the houses, while four of the seven night shelter workers said much the same thing about their views on running the night shelter. Similar proportions in both groups felt that the Director was not interested in utilizing their knowledge of residents in the houses and in the night shelter.

As in the earlier surveys of St Mungo staff, interaction of workers was greatest at the level of other workers, less with group leaders, and least with management. By contrast with the previous surveys, however, there was much less uniformity of opinion among the workers about group leaders, some of whom were seen as very helpful, rather than simply as 'a part' of management. There was a good deal of complaint, among house and night shelter workers, about the difficulty of getting into contact with the Director, the scarcity of information concerning what was going on in the organization and the lack of support from management.

Seven house workers left the St Mungo Community during or shortly following the period of the 1976 survey. Two were dismissed, two resigned in protest against the dismissals, two left because of disillusionment, and one for personal reasons. Other workers joined a union in order to try to bargain collectively with management. Comments from the workers were often couched in strong terms. Some feared intimidation. One said: 'In theory I should like to have more time for discussion with the Director, but, in practice, being aware of the way he would react to such situations, I would prefer to have no contact with him at all. It would only bring havoc and unhappiness on the house and tremendous strain on my fellow workers.' Another said: 'Consultation doesn't exist, which is best, as the kind of consultation that would come into consideration wouldn't be of a constructive kind. The only times I have heard or seen the Director, it has only been him shouting and swearing, and no-one else has got an opportunity to say what he thinks.' A third comment by a worker was: 'I feel it would be pointless to express a view, because one gets the feeling that, (a) it would be misinterpreted and, (b) it would be flattened'. A fourth worker, asked to say why he had rated the general staff morale as he did, wrote on the schedule: 'Because of the feeling that the workers are treated more or less like dirt by the Director. In particular, that one is in grave danger of losing one's job if opinions are strongly expressed which are not in line with the Director's wishes.'

House workers were, in general, agreed that communication between themselves and the management was inadequate and that this led to inefficiency.

'Because we are never informed of, or consulted about, policy decisions, we feel it is pointless to make long-term plans for the house. For example, what is the point in encouraging the residents to paint the outside of the house if we may suddenly be given 24 hours notice that the builders will be arriving to re-do it so that it is done "professionally"? We were the ones who had to implement the quick clearance of [a particular house] for redecorating. We were given less than a week's notice. The residents there felt very unsettled about the whole thing and obviously find it difficult to believe that the workers are as much in the dark about future plans for their house as they themselves are.'

One worker cited six reasons for the anxiety he expressed at his interview:

'(1) There is no response at all, from the management, to effort and/or ideas coming from the workers; (2) There is a very serious lack of job security resulting from sackings and/or resignations of workers who have quite evidently been having great success with residents but who may have had personality conflicts with the management; (3) It is impossible to think on a long-term basis in terms of one's own job; (4) The working situation can often become one where the worker is constantly worried, through the management's activities, more about the efficiency of paperwork than the welfare of the men; (5) There is a general feeling that the destiny of one's own position, of other workers, and even of the houses, is out of one's own control; (6) There is a serious staff shortage but no management support to compensate.'

Another worker gave an illustration of the common complaint that
it was difficult to get concrete and firm answers to questions about
practical issues from the management. He said:

> 'I have asked a senior member of staff at least six times in the past
> year for the exact figure of the house budget. The answer is always
> "they haven't sorted it out yet", or "at the moment I haven't got
> the information for that". The only exact figure I have is the
> housekeeping quota we collect weekly. I have vaguely heard there
> are two other budgets re house repairs, i.e. general repairs and
> major repairs. The definition of either has never been given to me
> even after repeated requests. I have heard arguments between
> senior staff regarding this but have never had an answer. If we
> knew more about budgeting we could get on with planning the
> economies management always insist upon.'

This lack of coherence and definition in policies was also said, by the
workers, to be characteristic of management decisions about residents: 'They are unconcerned about the welfare of the men in
consideration of staffing needs throughout the Community. When
re-planning they shuffle staff round like men on a chessboard to make
the picture balance and ignore the requirements of specific situations.'

Another type of complaint made by the workers about management was that it was 'unprofessional'. This illustrates the extent to
which the workers themselves had changed.

> 'A senior member of management runs down staff behind their
> backs to other members of the Community. There is a total absence
> of professional etiquette amongst senior members though they are
> quick to come down on junior staff for absence of such. Meetings
> never begin on time. They can be up to two or three hours late on
> occasions. Group leaders are bad in communicating information to
> house workers and sometimes don't even inform them when they
> are going on leave.'

As against these comments may be placed the view of the Director,
who suggested that within the limitations of the various agreements
made by the St Mungo Community with funding agencies, the
provisions of which were rigid, workers had a chance:

> 'to express their views and opinions and it is fair to say that in the
> last six months, and especially in the future, they have had and will

have a better opportunity to put forward constructive ideas and suggestions for serious discussion. This has arisen as we are now more stable, especially with regard to financing, and hopefully have more room for flexibility and experimentation. For example, all too often in the past, and because of the restrictions already mentioned and because of the complexity of the financing, we have had to rigidly stick to original agreements and have had to turn down suggestions which would have deviated from them, resulting in us being regarded as authoritarian and dictatorial. It is also my personal opinion that the confines of the action research project have been detrimental in certain areas to actually being able to provide the necessary ancillary services to ensure successful containment and possible rehabilitation of destitute men; one major example was the inability of the DHSS to adopt both our own and the research team's proposals for a workshop which, without doubt, was an integral and essential part of the success of this project. The value of such workshops is clearly demonstrated and has been known to DHSS for some time as all new reception centres have such facilities built into them.'

The Director was optimistic about the future of the organization: 'I see hope. I believe the Community has learned and is very much learning, but has now identified problem areas of worker management and is attempting to develop new skills to assist with it. By that, a greater education of the senior workers in their particular jobs to assist more the day-to-day worker in their particular job.'

By the summer of 1976, the crisis that the St Mungo Community had undergone during the spring was over. The most vocal critics of management had been dismissed or had resigned and it appeared that the organization would experience a further period of calm. The main work of the research team came to an end at this point.

Discussion

Within this outline of events it is possible to distinguish many of the themes already discussed. The workers (although they did not use the terminology) suggested that management was 'guilty' of a 'displacement of goals', and felt that, in its concern for the wellbeing of the organization, it had lost sight of its original purpose. The workers believed, too, that the objectives of management were becoming increasingly divorced from the 'particularistic' ideology which had been the stimulus for the organization's foundation. Management, in its agreements with external funding agencies, tended to emphasize 'universalistic' values which would secure wide support and were amenable to compromise.

As the St Mungo Community increased in size it experienced the process of organizational development described by Michels. The roles of management and workers became separated and the tasks of administration were increasingly taken over by specialized staff. The power of decision-making was delegated, because of the increasing size and complexity of the organization, and came to be vested in a small management group. Each crisis was characterized by complaints, from the workers, about arbitrary and undemocratic management actions. The St Mungo Community (whose management, in early pamphlets, had emphasized the importance of egalitarianism and collective decision-making) came to be seen by the workers as an authoritarian oligarchy.

In drawing attention to the correspondence between developments within the St Mungo Community and those in other voluntary organizations we do not suggest that the outcome of these events was inevitable. The consequence of some policies could, of course, in general terms, be predicted. A policy of rapid organizational expansion was likely to result in a diminution in collective decision-making, and it was to be expected, given the history and the ideology of the organization, that the decision to enter into an agreement with a government department would result in resistance and resentment on the part of many workers. While some consequences of policy could be predicted, however, the particular reactions of management and workers to the stresses resulting from this policy could not.

Workers and management sometimes acted in ways that were at variance with the 'model' of their roles presented at the beginning of the section. On each occasion of crisis, for example, workers complained that management actions were arbitrary. If this were the case (and the complaint seemed to have substance), a designation of the management as bureaucratic, in Weber's sense, would have to be qualified. Weber emphasized the uniformity and continuity of policy within bureaucracies. Similarly, the criticisms made by some workers in 1976 (that the management's behaviour was erratic, ill-planned, and inefficient), might have been those of bureaucrats whose work was frustrated by the capriciousness of a charismatic leader.

Moreover, the views of workers and management, although divergent, were not completely divorced. The staff interviews indicated that many workers (even in the early phases of the research project) accepted the need for some delegation of decision-making. Similarly the pleas of many workers in 1976 for greater efficiency within the organization and a more 'professional' approach to the problems of the residents echoed those that the management had been making for several years. The crux of the disagreement between the two groups was only partly concerned with the content of policy. In part, too, the workers' grievances arose from the manner in which policy was formulated.

The most persistent complaint of the workers, on each occasion of crisis, was that they were given no opportunity to discuss the changes that were taking place. Policy decisions were usually issued as directives and workers were given the option of accepting them or resigning. This was the case, for example, with the termination of the workers' participation in the soup run. Many workers experienced a feeling of powerlessness and felt that they lacked any control over the decisions that affected their work. This was an important reason for the low morale they often expressed. In particular, they felt disheartened at not being able to justify policy to the residents. Many who resigned questioned their own usefulness, believing that the progress they had made in helping residents might be nullified by a sudden management decision. Workers complained, for example, that unsuitable transfers of residents (from house to house), were ordered by members of the management who hardly knew the men concerned.

Since the views of workers and management were not totally different it seemed possible that many of the disputes that occurred might have been settled if the latter had been prepared to accept the possibility of compromise. Management seemed unwilling, however, to adopt a more conciliatory attitude. Their views concerning decision-making changed little during the period of the research project. In part, this might have been due to isolation from the houses. Senior members of management met residents infrequently and relied on 'intermediate' staff (the Group Leaders) to implement their policies. The workers had to cope daily with the problems involved in caring for (and living with) the residents. Their role was exhausting, entailed a high level of responsibility without power, and sometimes seemed thankless. In these circumstances, they were prepared to revise ideas that seemed irrelevant to the practical problems involved in caring for the men, and would have appreciated more management involvement in their work. In view of the difficulties they experienced in communicating with management, the formation of a union branch seemed, to many, a necessary development. They hoped that a recognized bargaining body, which could negotiate disputes, would reduce the power differential between themselves and management and perhaps encourage compromise.

The St Mungo Community in 1976 bore little resemblance to the organization that was founded in 1969. The original workers (none of whom remained apart from the Director) joined the organization in order to affirm an alternative life-style. To some extent they were motivated by a rejection of society at that time. The workers in 1976 did not share this motivation. Their views were more pragmatic, they tended to have more professional qualifications, and their energies were directed towards working for change within, rather than outside, conventional society. Their decision to apply for trade union membership reflected this. The management–worker dispute was no longer concerned with the interpretation of a 'particularistic' doctrine. The conflict was more about bargaining power and employee security. Thus an article in a national newspaper reported the Director as saying: 'We couldn't pay the union's going rate . . . if we had to pay people at union levels we'd just have to close' (Daily Telegraph 1977a). The article prompted a letter from an official of the Association of Clerical, Technical and Supervisory staff (ACTS), criticizing it for 'errors of fact' and suggesting that, in the interests of a balanced portrayal of the situation, the reporter should have consulted '. . . the other parties to the issue, the employees, including those judged to have been unfairly dismissed' (Daily Telegraph 1977b). Disputes of this kind (probably more amenable to compromise than the ideological quarrels of previous years) were indicative of the ways in which the St Mungo Community had changed.

The influence of the research team

The point of an action research project is to allow the research team to contribute to the formulation of policy and practice, but it is essential that this be done in a specific and restricted way. We put forward a number of recommendations at intervals, explaining in detail to management and staff the reasons for making them, but also emphasizing our awareness that actual policy decisions could only be taken by management. In fact several of our recommendations were not accepted. One of our major assumptions, frequently made explicit, was that the power of St Mungo's to help destitute men stemmed as much from the motivation of the workers on the soup run, in the night shelter, and in the houses, as from the organization of the service they provided. The recommendations that workers should take part in decision making (Chapter 4, p. 60) and that the soup run should be strengthened (Chapter 4, p. 58) were designed to capitalize on this motivation. The increase in professional expertise that resulted from our recommendations concerning skilled group leaders and a regular assessment routine did not lessen this motivation (although the underlying ideologies changed considerably) but actually made it more effective.

Workers appreciated the opportunity to formulate their problems in confidential discussion with the research team and this may have fostered their own intercommunication and determination to resist what they regarded as authoritarian practices. In general, however, when the history of similar organizations is taken into account, it seems unlikely that the presence of the research team made much difference to the events described in this chapter. The conflicts between management and workers had other origins.

In Chapter 6 we shall consider the changes at St Mungo's from a different perspective by comparing the views and attitudes of the St Mungo staff with those of staff in the Camberwell Reception Centre and the small London reception centres for destitute men. Our intention in doing so was to assess the extent to which attributed differences between statutory and voluntary agencies for the destitute, discussed in Chapter 1, were in fact borne out.

Summary

The conflicts that beset the Simon Community are perhaps inherent in any organization whose ends are idealistic but whose means are limited, particularly when one of the ideals is that of free participation of all members in decision-making and collective responsibility for policy. The different Simon Communities tended to go in different directions, some striving to keep the original ideals undiluted, others looking for a model in professional social work. Similar tendencies could be seen in the St Mungo Community at different times. The main conflict, however, developed between workers, on the one hand,

and management on the other. Behind this conflict lay the undoubted problems of an expanding organization, with an increasing tendency towards bureaucracy and central direction. Constraints were set up by the organization's need to maintain funds from government departments and local authorities, and in such a situation the ideas and enthusiasm of young workers might often have seemed naive and unrestrained to those who had been with the St Mungo Community from the beginning, and had, to some extent at least, lost their original idealism.

The possibility of a crisis developing within the organization was clearly evident during the time of the pilot survey and it seemed possible, during that period, that either of two tendencies within the St Mungo Community (one towards trying out every theory, no matter how fanciful, in the hope of helping destitute men, and one towards developing into an authoritarian type of institution supplying accommodation of a lodging house kind) could, if allowed free rein, result in the destruction of the whole enterprise. The crisis came in October 1972 when a substantial proportion of workers left the organization. As new workers replaced the most outspoken critics, the wounds began to heal, and there followed nearly three years of relative calm. Although the same tensions between the workers and management were apparent below the surface these did not result in overt conflict, partly, perhaps, because few workers remained who had been with the St Mungo Community from its beginnings.

The organization continued to expand its services, particularly the night shelter and the 'lodging house' accommodation in the former Charing Cross Hospital, which undoubtedly did offer extra help, not otherwise available. The overall policy of the management became more obviously directed towards developing a large-scale service of the 'casual' type. House workers again began to resist, but this time from a basis of greater experience and training. One complaint made by many workers in 1976 referred to a lack of professionalism in management and an important development was the formation, by some workers, of a union branch to represent staff interests. It was hoped that a recognized bargaining body, which could negotiate disputes with management, would tend towards an equalization of power within the organization and so enhance the chances of compromise in disputes. The outcome of these events was still uncertain when the research project came to an end.

6 Comparisons between voluntary and statutory services

Attributed differences at the start of the research programme

In Chapters 1 and 2, we discussed the evolution of government policies for dealing with destitution and, in particular, the substantial changes in general approach that accompanied the social reforms of the late 1940s and early 1950s. At that time it was anticipated that most destitution would be prevented by strengthening the supportive apparatus of the welfare state in fields such as education, employment, housing, and pensions, and by making more specific benefits and help available to the disadvantaged and disabled. It was thought that these measures would ensure that the group of people who still became chronically destitute would be small enough to be dealt with by local medical and social services. By the mid-1960s, however, it was clear that things were not going according to plan. Piecemeal social welfare policies were not coping adequately with disadvantaged groups, disabled people (particularly psychiatric patients) were not receiving adequate community care, and the supply of cheap accommodation in rented rooms and lodging houses was decreasing more rapidly than the demand. The numbers of men using reception centres increased, and in the run-down areas of large cities substantial numbers of people were sleeping rough. Although the intention to move away from Poor Law policies was central to government planning, and substantial progress had been made, it was difficult to argue that all vestiges had been eradicated when the fabric of Poor Law institutions (notably in the Camberwell Reception Centre) remained so evidently present.

In these circumstances, criticisms by the new voluntary social work movement had considerable public impact. Some critics claimed to offer a completely new approach, both in theory and practice, and suggested that the statutory services had remained, in all essentials, mid-Victorian. Other critics were more moderate and argued only that they were providing a new type of service for men who were not attracted by the old. The supposed disparity of approach and practice between statutory and voluntary services was a source of much debate.

Attitudes of staff at Camberwell Reception Centre and St Mungo's

The research team made a series of simple ratings of the attitudes of workers at St Mungo's in order to assess whether they changed over time and, if so, what factors might determine the changes. Some results were described in Chapter 5. A similar survey was carried out at the Camberwell Reception Centre with the agreement of staff and management there. Interviews in both settings were conducted during March and April 1973 and, for present purposes, only staff who had been in post for more than three months will be considered. At Camberwell, all senior staff, and a sample of one in two assistants, were interviewed (N60), and at the Battersea Annexe* all nine eligible staff were included. At St Mungo's, all twenty-nine staff were interviewed.

* This annexe (formerly the Battersea Hospital) accommodated about seventy elderly residents. In comparison with the Camberwell Reception Centre, the building was small and its grounds were pleasantly landscaped with lawns, trees and flowerbeds. Eight or ten residents shared each dormitory at the Annexe and the residents were allowed to decorate the space surrounding their beds with photographs and other objects. The rather depressing appearance of some dormitories at the Camberwell Reception Centre (which contained long lines of beds and seemed empty of personal belongings) was not characteristic of the Battersea accommodation. Most of the residents at the Battersea Annexe were specially selected from among the elderly, long-term residents at the Camberwell Reception Centre.

The St Mungo staff were younger than staff at the Camberwell Reception Centre (50 per cent were aged thirty or under compared with 19 per cent of staff at the Centre), more likely to be female (31 per cent compared with 2 per cent), and more likely to have O-levels or other educational qualifications (73 per cent compared with 29 per cent; reflecting, in part, the difference in age between the two groups of staff and, therefore, the difference in educational opportunity). The St Mungo staff were less experienced in working with destitute men than staff at the Camberwell Reception Centre (10 per cent of the St Mungo staff had been working in the field for two years or more compared with 65 per cent of staff at the Centre) and less likely to see their future in terms of this kind of work (48 per cent of the St Mungo staff wanted to stay for at least two years altogether in their present job compared with 94 per cent of staff at the Centre). Staff at the Camberwell Reception Centre generally saw themselves remaining as long as possible in their present job. Many staff at the Centre pointed out the advantages of job security and the emotional rewards of a job that assisted the disadvantaged. The St Mungo workers usually experienced their work as emotionally rewarding but exhausting due to the long hours they worked and the 'commitment' required by the job. The workers usually felt that one or two years living with the residents, with little time off, was a reasonable period.

Questions were asked by the research team about the morale of members of these groups of staff, both individually and as it was seen among the staff as a whole. Individual morale was high in both settings (79 per cent of St Mungo staff gave themselves a rating of 6 or more for morale on a scale with a low of 1 and a high of 9, compared with 88 per cent of the staff at the Centre). However, St Mungo staff were more likely to give a high rating of staff morale as a whole than were staff at the Camberwell Reception Centre (65 per cent compared with 39 per cent). On several questions about attitudes to the organization (whether it was helpful, permissive, integrated with the general community, innovative, etc.) staff in both settings were equally favourable, but when asked how members of the general public would answer these questions St Mungo staff supposed that the public view of St Mungo's would be the same as their own, while Camberwell staff thought that the public view of the reception centre would be distinctly unfavourable.

In general, questions concerning the degree of interaction between staff of all grades in the respective organizations revealed greater staff interaction at the St Mungo Community than at the Camberwell Reception Centre. (At St Mungo's staff lived-in but there were regular business meetings and duty on the soup run.) Interaction between staff was obviously more common among those at the same level. This was true of both organizations. Staff interaction was greater in the St Mungo Community than at the Camberwell Reception Centre at all staff levels with the exception that somewhat more staff at the Centre thought the Manager/Director of their organization was accessible and easy to contact (85 per cent of Centre staff compared with 74 per cent of St Mungo staff).

Both groups of staff thought that their work had made them more understanding of the problems of destitute men and there was little difference between them in this respect. The general attitudes of these groups of staff to destitution were also enquired into by the research team. On the whole, there was considerable agreement in attitudes between the St Mungo staff and the staff at the Centre. The large majority of staff in both organizations thought, for example, that destitute men were often handicapped, that insufficient cheap accommodation was available, that destitute men would prefer to live in decent accommodation if they could afford it, that these men did not deserve rejection by society, and that they would work if they could obtain employment. However, the St Mungo staff were rather more optimistic about the prospects of helping destitute men than were staff at the Camberwell Reception Centre. None of the St Mungo staff agreed with the statement that it was no use offering destitute men anything better, since they preferred to live in poor conditions. Twenty per cent of staff at the Centre agreed with this. The St Mungo staff were also less ready than staff at the Centre to agree that destitute men were likely to remain unemployed for the rest of their lives, irrespective of any help provided for them (11 per cent of St Mungo staff compared with 27 per cent of staff at the Centre). The St Mungo staff were more inclined than staff at the Centre to consider that society was to blame for the condition of destitute men.

Staff from the respective organizations were asked their views concerning the responsibilities that could be undertaken by residents. The St Mungo staff tended to favour a higher level of resident responsibility than staff at the Centre. A higher proportion of the St Mungo staff, for example, thought that residents had a right to vote on staff decisions affecting them and that residents should decide for themselves whether or not they were ready to begin work. On the other hand, the St Mungo staff were less ready than the staff at the Centre to support a system of compulsory in-house tasks which residents should be obliged to perform.

Only nine members of staff at the Battersea Annexe were interviewed by the research team (the Annexe employs relatively few staff because of its small size) but the results of the interviews are included because of their potential interest.

The characteristics of the Battersea staff tended to be intermediate between those of the St Mungo and the Camberwell Reception Centre staff. This was true of the length of employment, likely future length of stay, education, and age. Many of the responses to questions concerning their working experiences were also intermediate between those of the St Mungo and Camberwell Reception Centre staff, although some responses were closer, if anything, to those of St Mungo staff. This was true, for example, of the opinions of Battersea staff about general staff morale and of most of their responses concerning staff interaction. An exception to the intermediate position was that the Manager of the Annexe appeared to interact more with his staff than did the leaders of the other two organizations.

When asked by the research team about resident responsibility, the Battersea staff had mixed views. The majority thought that residents should be allowed to attend staff meetings but that they should not be given responsibilities in the Annexe. None of the Battersea staff, for example, were in favour of residents having their own key to the Annexe. The staff at the Annexe saw some destitute men as being handicapped, were optimistic of some measure of rehabilitation for destitute men if suitable help was provided and thought it would be wrong if society were to reject such men because of 'antisocial characteristics'. The greater optimism of staff at the Battersea Annexe *vis-à-vis* staff at the Camberwell Reception Centre concerning the prospects of helping destitute men may be due, in part, to differences in the type of resident the two groups of staff deal with. Residents at the Camberwell Reception Centre show a higher incidence of physical and mental disability than residents at the Battersea Annexe and require more specialized help. Residents at the Annexe, because of their age, are also more likely to be found Part III accommodation in due course, as it becomes slowly available.

These differences between Camberwell and St Mungo staff are by no means as large as might have been expected from the different character of the organizations. The research team suggested that changes could be made in the way that reception centres operated without necessarily incurring the displeasure of reception centre staff and that the potential existed in the statutory services to combine aspects of voluntary and statutory provision. The Battersea Annexe illustrated this potential. The senior staff of the Annexe were professionally trained and had considerable experience of working with destitute men. The Annexe was large enough to enable a wide range of facilities to be available to its residents, including quite extensive gardens for occupational and leisure use. It was small enough, however, to allow frequent interaction between residents and staff. The maintenance of a structured yet personal regime was a stated aim of the Battersea staff. The quality of the Annexe environment, as experienced by its residents, was intermediate between that of the St Mungo Community and the Camberwell Reception Centre, just as the Annexe was intermediate in size. From this finding it seemed likely that the DHSS policy of building smaller reception centres would produce environments different in degree rather than in kind to those of the St Mungo Community and similar voluntary organizations.

Characteristics of men at Camberwell and St Mungo's who had stayed more than three months

At about the same time as the interviews with staff in the two settings a survey of 'residents' was also carried out. All thirty-eight men who had been in St Mungo houses for three months or more on 1 April 1973, with the exception of two who refused, one who was discharged before he could be seen, and five who might have become upset if questioned, were interviewed. Data about these men were compared with those from equivalent interviews with a 1:2 sample of men who had been resident at the Camberwell Reception Centre for at least three months on 1 February 1973. The comparisons made are summarized in *Table 6(1)*.

St Mungo residents were older but likely to have stayed for a shorter time. Most personal and social characteristics, including indices of destitution, were similar in the two groups. There were marked differences, however, in attitudes to the social environment.

Table 6(1):   *Characteristics and attitudes of men staying in Camberwell Reception Centre and St Mungo houses for more than three months (1973)*

characteristic	Camberwell 1.2.1973 (N50) %	St Mungo's 1.4.1973 (N30) %
aged over 50 years	46	71*
born in England and Wales	66	77
resident over one year	46	13†
never married	66	70
ever in psychiatric hospital	38	20
ever in prison	63	46
ever problem with alcohol	30	15
asked for suggestions by staff	8	38†
talks to staff often	22	76†
thinks staff appear friendly	45	93‡
thinks other residents have similar problems	19	61‡
satisfied with food	42	72*
satisfied with sleeping accommodation	70	87
satisfied with atmosphere	33	70†
wants to stay as long as possible	36	64†
would prefer accommodation in digs	40	17†
feels he is unlikely to become independent	43	50

*$p<.05$ †$p<.01$ ‡$p<.001$

Staff at St Mungo's were regarded as more friendly and more accessible and the amenities were described as more satisfactory. Men at St Mungo's were more likely to want to stay and less likely to accept a suggestion that accommodation in digs would be preferable. In addition, St Mungo residents were more likely than residents at Camberwell to say that other men had similar problems to their own.

The fact that attitudes to staff at St Mungo's were more positive suggests that the attitudes of staff themselves, which were not very different in the two settings, might have been affected, in the case of Camberwell, by a social desirability factor, i.e. an awareness of the standards generally valued by other people. However, the influence of the Camberwell buildings and amenities must also be taken into account. The attitudes of men at the smaller reception centres would be relevant to the explanation adopted and these will be considered in a subsequent section.

A further survey of men staying three months or more in St Mungo houses was carried out in April 1976, when the process of accumulation described in Chapter 4 was complete. The results are shown (for convenience of comparison with other data) in *Table 6(3)* on page 141. The men in the later survey were longer-stay and more likely to have been in psychiatric hospitals, in these respects coming closer to men at Camberwell. Their responses to staff and amenities are less positive, though still better than in the earlier survey of Camberwell. Further discussion will be deferred until other comparative data have been presented.

Comparison between characteristics of men at Camberwell, St Mungo's, and two smaller reception centres

It was suggested in Chapters 4 and 5 that both management policies and staff practices at St Mungo's became, over the years, less and less clearly differentiated from the policy and practice of statutory services, although a number of unimportant distinctions remained. The differences had probably never been as great as was claimed, as the attitude study reported in the previous section suggests. At the same time, the reception centre system had experienced developments which reduced these differences. The lease of the large Camberwell centre is due to expire in the 1980s and it was planned to replace it by smaller centres, several of which have already opened. In addition to definite plans for three new centres, the Supplementary Benefits Commission is engaged in negotiations to use part of the Poplar Hospital in Tower Hamlets as a centre to accommodate between 120 and 150 people. It is hoped that this, together with a proposed new purpose-built centre on the site of the Battersea Centre in Wandsworth, will provide all that is needed to replace the beds lost by the proposed closure of Camberwell.

Two of the new centres – Pound Lodge in Willesden and Cedars Lodge in Clapham – were selected for study (with the agreement of

management and staff) because they offered an opportunity to test the
ideas originating from the work at Camberwell and St Mungo's.

Two small reception centres

Pound Lodge was opened in October 1973. Men in need of its services
are admitted to the centre directly from the streets. It has eighty-five
beds, thirty-six of which are for 'casual' admissions, forty-nine for
men taken into 'residence'. Medical help for the men is provided by a
doctor (who holds a surgery three times weekly) and a nurse who
works each weekday from 9–5pm. The centre has a five-bed sick bay
and a one-bed isolation room. A workshop provides the men with
opportunities for carpentry and painting.

Cedars Lodge was opened in June 1973 and accommodates both
men and women. Only the men were of concern to the research. Men
whose motivation for resettlement appears good are referred from the
Camberwell Reception Centre by one of its Executive Officers after
consultation with Cedars Lodge staff. Cedars Lodge houses about
seventy men and twenty-five women. About 400 men are admitted
each year. A general practitioner attends the centre for two 2-hour
sessions each week and a nurse, working a forty-hour week, is
available every day, from Monday to Friday. There is a five-bed sick
bay. A workshop providing facilities for light woodwork was opened
in 1974 and men are employed in cultivating and maintaining the
extensive grounds.

Neither centre has the rather grim, institutional appearance of
Camberwell. They are much smaller, have attractively laid out
grounds and blend fairly well into the surrounding district. Pound
Lodge, situated in a busy, highly populated area of North London, is
surrounded by streets of identical terraced houses and numerous
small factories and workshops. Cedars Lodge, situated in an attractive tree-lined road near Clapham Common, forms part of a fairly
prosperous district of large houses and hotels.

These particular centres were selected for study because their
admission procedures (and therefore perhaps their clienteles) were
rather different. Pound Lodge had no selection procedure, taking men
directly from the streets if their circumstances were such that they
seemed in need of a reception centre's services. The Cedars Lodge
men, on the other hand, were a selected group from the Camberwell
Reception Centre.

The aim of both centres was to assist the men contacting them to find employment and accommodation in the community. Neither centre was visited by a DRO but each had a good relationship with the local employment exchange. Seven or eight Cedars Lodge residents worked on the Peter Bedford scheme which utilized short-life London Borough accommodation as housing, engaged the men in cleaning work, and attempted to provide a place for them to live after 'apprenticeship' and some staff support. There was also a close relationship with the ten-bed alcoholic unit (Kenwood Hall) run by the Helping Hand organization; otherwise hostel and bed-sitter accommodation was not linked with the centres.

Three hypotheses were put forward which entailed a comparison between data collected at Camberwell in 1973, at St Mungo's in 1976, and in the two new centres in 1977–8. The validity of making such comparisons will be discussed later.

The first hypothesis was that the characteristics of the men using the various services, particularly those of men who remained in residence for three months or more, would be very similar. In particular, they would be chronically disabled as well as socially disadvantaged. The second hypothesis was that the attitudes of men towards the staff and towards the amenities provided at the two smaller centres would be more similar to the attitudes of men at St Mungo's than to those of men at Camberwell. The third hypothesis was that the outcome after discharge would reflect the disabilities of the men rather than any differences in environment or regime that might be found between the organizations.

Three surveys were carried out at the two smaller reception centres, as follows:

(i) *A case-paper survey*   In order to obtain minimal data on all the men contacting the centres, information was recorded from the case-papers of a random sample of men admitted during the year 1 April 1976–31 March 1977. About a hundred men were surveyed at each centre. At Pound Lodge a one in seven sample produced 102 cases, at Cedars Lodge a one in three sample produced 108. Attempts were made to derive basic social and medical data for each of these men (e.g. age, birthplace, marital status, experience of hospitalization). Inevitably some data were missing or were judged to be too vague or incomplete to be utilized. For this reason it was not always possible to generalize from the findings. On the whole, however, the data were satisfactory for our purposes.

(ii) Interviews with selected residents   Residents who had stayed at each centre for at least three months were interviewed. About thirty men were seen at each centre. At Cedars Lodge, men who completed a period of residence of at least three months were selected for interview. Their stay at Camberwell prior to their current Cedars Lodge admission was included when calculating this period.* Thirty-four out of the thirty-five men in this group were seen. At Pound Lodge, men who had completed a period of residence of at least three months were selected for interview. Thirty of the thirty-seven men in this group were seen. The seven men who were not interviewed left the centre very soon after the expiry of the three-month period and before an interview could be arranged. The schedules used to guide the interviews were similar to those used at the Camberwell Reception Centre in 1973 and the St Mungo Community in 1976.

(iii) A follow-up enquiry   In order to determine the proportion of residents being resettled in their own accommodation a follow-up enquiry into the whereabouts of men leaving the centres was undertaken. This involved four groups of men: the two case-paper groups and the two interviewed groups described in (i) and (ii) above. Efforts were made to trace these men two, four and six months after their departure from the centres. To this end, enquiries were made at London reception centres, voluntary bodies, and other agencies (e.g. the NAVH). The Department also circulated a list of untraced interviewed men to reception centres outside London.

A summary of the characteristics of the case-paper groups and the interviewed groups at the two smaller centres is presented in *Table 6(2)*.

The differences between the case-paper groups are presumably due to the fact that men from Camberwell who are thought suitable for rehabilitation and resettlement are selected for transfer to Cedars

---

* Men who had stayed in Cedars Lodge at least three months at the time of interview (N19) were more likely to have been born in England and Wales, to have married, and to have slept rough. In other respects the characteristics of this group were similar to those who had spent part of the three months at Camberwell.

Table 6(2):   *Characteristics of men in the case-paper and interviewed groups at Pound Lodge and Cedars Lodge*

characteristic	Pound Lodge		Cedars Lodge	
	case-paper (N102) %	interviewed (N30) %	case-paper (N108) %	interviewed (N34) %
aged over 50 years	12	37	11	41
born in England and Wales	45	43	45	32
resident over one year	3	27	13	24
never married	70	63	55	47
ever in psychiatric hospital	21	50	35	59
ever in prison	27	30	45	62
ever problem with alcohol	27	46	55	41

Lodge while men at Pound Lodge are admitted directly. The former group are more likely to have been married but also more likely to have been in prison or psychiatric hospital and to have had a problem with alcohol.* Considering only those who have been resident for three months or more (the interviewed group), there are very few differences; in fact only the larger proportion of longer-term men at Cedars Lodge who have been in prison remains significant. (This is probably due to the selection process, since Camberwell is known to have a higher proportion of ex-offenders than other reception centres.) Those who stay for three months or more at Pound Lodge are more likely to have a history of alcohol problems, prison or psychiatric hospital than the case-paper group, and the latter two items also become more concentrated in the interviewed group at Cedars Lodge. At both centres, age has a marked selective effect, the younger men being more likely to be discharged before they have stayed three months. There was insufficient information in the case-papers to make it worthwhile comparing previous occupation or

---

*Since this study was completed, a more deliberate policy of selecting elderly and mentally disabled men for transfer to Cedars Lodge has been adopted. The difference is therefore likely to have increased even further.

length of time sleeping rough. Better information was available from the interviewed groups and accorded well with the data provided by the case-papers.

The interviewed men were asked a series of standard questions about their relationship with staff, their satisfaction with amenities and their views on future accommodation. The questions had been used in the earlier studies at Camberwell and St Mungo's and were asked in the same neutral way, so that men should not feel there was any pressure towards a particular type of answer. The answers reflect their subjective opinions and we were not able to check their validity objectively.

Some representative comments made by men at the two smaller centres are quoted to illustrate their attitudes and allow some comparison with what has earlier been said about Camberwell and St Mungo's. There were no marked differences between the two centres in the men's reported interactions with, or attitudes to, staff. Few men said that the staff had ever asked them for suggestions concerning the running of the centres (7 per cent and 9 per cent), although approximately a third of each group thought that staff would seriously consider any suggestions they might make (Pound Lodge 33 per cent, Cedars Lodge 41 per cent). 'If you have any problems you're always free to knock at the manager's door', one man commented. Another felt that, 'They would listen and try and understand your views on the matter. Nine times out of ten they probably wouldn't do anything. It would depend on how many people made the suggestion.' About a third of each group said that they talked to staff often. Some men said that they had conversations with staff 'every day'. Others exchanged the 'usual civilities' (as one resident expressed it) of 'good morning' and 'hello'. When asked how they regarded staff the great majority of men gave a favourable response. Typical remarks were 'They're all respectable people'; 'very pleasant and hardworking'; 'on the whole very good'; 'I think they're doing a good job'. One man said, 'If you're polite to them, they're polite to you. They are very understanding and very helpful. Altogether a hundred per cent better than Camberwell is.' Another commented, 'If you're genuine about things they listen to you and try to help. Mr . . ., in particular, has been very good to me. He's a genuine man.' Some men, while feeling that the staff were, on the whole, good, made the point that it was difficult to generalize about them. One said specifically that there was a good deal of variation and complained that some staff members tended to adopt a threatening tone which he thought went beyond their authority. Few men, however, held markedly hostile feelings towards staff. Those that did often felt that they were 'two-faced'. 'They smile and call you by your Christian name and it all goes down in the book.' The men at Cedars Lodge were more likely than those at Pound Lodge to say that they had received assistance from staff in finding work (41 per cent compared with 17 per cent).

When asked to give an opinion about amenities at the centres the majority of men expressed feelings of satisfaction. The cleanliness of the sleeping accommodation came in for particular praise. In one man's opinion it was 'lovely. I've never had better for years and years'. Another remarked approvingly, 'you can see it for yourself'. 83 per cent of men at Pound Lodge and 91 per cent of those at Cedars Lodge rated the sleeping accommodation as good. Rather fewer men were satisfied with the food (Pound Lodge 60 per cent, Cedars Lodge 74 per cent), and fewer still with the centres' atmosphere (Pound Lodge 50 per cent, Cedars Lodge 59 per cent). The most common complaints about the food were that it was insufficient and that menus were repetitive. One unemployed man, who felt that the quantity of food could be increased, commented, 'It would be no use if you were working' [i.e. insufficient to sustain heavy physical work]. Others, while stating that the quantity and quality of the food left something to be desired, felt that it was as good as they could reasonably expect. 'There could be improvements but, considering the number they have to cook for, it is good.' The atmosphere of the centres was most commonly criticized on three counts. Men found the rules of the organizations restrictive, their environments drab and boring and were upset and annoyed by the behaviour of other inmates. One man, with an alcohol problem, who was attempting to 'stay dry' and whose nerves were 'very shaky' described his centre as 'very rough. The atmosphere is partially violent. There are quite a few brawls here. I work in the kitchen here washing-up. I don't like it, I feel it's not helping my nerves. I can't cope with the job, that's all.' Another man described the atmosphere as: 'Not too bad. Sometimes people make too much noise. There's not the staff. Sometimes you wonder where you can go for a bit of peace and quiet.' A third commented:

'I'll have to move soon, my nerves are so bad. This is not classed surely as a mental home? I thought it was a reception centre. I'm beginning to wonder. I do think they should grade people. I don't see why we should have to sleep next to these people [residents with psychiatric disabilities]. The actual living here is a vegetable life as far as I'm concerned. I wash-up in the kitchen. On my shift you can't see TV and they don't change the shifts round.'

The views of some other residents were more favourable than this. A few seemed to derive stimulation from the large numbers of men they came into contact with. 'Considering that there are over a hundred of us I think it is . . . [a pause] . . . it fluctuates. Not depressing. It's anti-depressing. I'd say a likeable atmosphere.'

A substantial proportion of men in both centres felt that, in their behaviour and situation, they were 'different' from other men there. Forty-three per cent of the Pound Lodge group and 35 per cent of those at Cedars Lodge felt that they had little in common with the other men. Many men emphasized that they were different from residents with psychiatric disabilities. One man said 'There are a lot of mental cases here. Two from a mental hospital used to creep about in the night. I've got a cubicle now. I asked to be taken out' [of his dormitory]. Another commented: 'There are so many people here who are mental. If I don't leave here soon I'll have a mental breakdown. It's asking too much.' Some men felt that other residents were 'morally' different, being untrustworthy, feckless, and lazy. One said of his fellow-inmates: 'They don't put themselves out to help you. They sit around all day. I like to keep active.' Another commented: 'They're one of every kind, they're very mixed. Some have been in prison. You couldn't take your watch off and leave it about. You choose your own kind. There are one or two decent types.' A third said, 'Other residents don't do any work. They get a voucher to go to the alcoholic unit at Camberwell and just sit around all day. What would happen if we all did that?' Other men took a different view and pointed to the common elements in the residents' situation. They felt that these outweighed any differences between the men. One commented, 'We're all out of work, we have no accommodation, no direct contact with relatives, even where there are any. We're all looking for the same thing, to pick up, to start afresh.' Another, when asked if he felt that the other residents had much in common with him, replied, 'Yes, I'm homeless and I have a problem with drinking.'

About half the men in both groups said they wanted to leave the centres quickly. This was more true of the Pound Lodge men (57 per cent compared with 47 per cent). The majority of those wanting to leave said that they would like to live in their own flat or digs (Pound Lodge 56 per cent, Cedars Lodge 62 per cent). Half the men, however, expressed no confidence in their ability to find and maintain independent accommodation. Many pointed to the difficulties of getting work. One man said 'In order to live in a place you have to have a job – to pay the rent. I don't think my job prospects are very good. I've been out of work for two years and that will go against me.' In some cases age and physical ill-health exacerbated these problems. A resident of sixty-two commented: 'It's finding a job that's difficult. At my age it's difficult. They don't want to know you.' Other men felt that they needed the support and structure of an institution if they were to cope with their problems. One man, when asked where he wanted to live, replied 'A cubicle here. How long are you going to keep your own room for? As soon as you miss the rent that's you out! If I was on my own I'd get fed-up. I'd be at the drinking. I want some discipline. Some people don't but I do.' Some men were anxious not to sever their links with the centres completely. One resident, who drank excessively when he got depressed and had a history of drinking offences, psychiatric admissions, and violence, was asked how confident he felt about his chances of getting a flat or digs. 'If I had the money I'm pretty confident whereas in the past I'd have been too frightened to. I'd have been frightened of people. I feel I can face the outside world now. I think the centre is one reason. I'd like to keep my contacts here in case things go wrong.' A few residents, however, were completely pessimistic about their future. One, very dejected at the interview, replied when asked if he would like to continue living in the centre, 'The only thing I can see in front of me is sleeping rough. I can't answer that question.' This man felt that he couldn't control his drinking without help and so couldn't hold down a job. He thought he might as well be in a reception centre as in a smaller hostel. Ideally he would have liked his own room but saw no hope of getting one. The Pound Lodge group tended to feel less confident than men at Cedars Lodge about the chances of finding and maintaining their own accommodation (57 per cent compared with 47 per cent).

A summary of data about men who had been resident for three months or more at the time of the surveys at Camberwell in 1973, St Mungo's in 1976, and the two smaller centres is given in *Table 6(3)*.

The men staying in Pound Lodge and Cedars Lodge in 1977 had rather different characteristics, in some respects, to those staying an

Table 6(3): Characteristics and attitudes of men staying in the Camberwell Reception Centre, the St Mungo Community, Pound Lodge and Cedars Lodge for three months or more

	CRC (1973) (N50) %	SMC (1976) (N59) %	Pound Lodge (1977) (N30) %	Cedars Lodge (1977) (N34) %
aged over 50	46	59	37	41
born in England or Wales	66	37	43	32
resident over one year	46	53	27	24
never married	66	68	63	47
slept rough 1 yr + at stretch	10	30	37	41
ever in psychiatric hospital	38	39	50	59
ever in prison	63	42	30	62
ever problem with alcohol	30	27	46	41
asked for suggestions by staff	8	12	7	9
talks to staff often	22	49	40	38
thinks staff appear friendly	45	86	97	85
thinks other residents have similar problems	19	46	43	35
satisfied with food	42	56	60	74
satisfied with sleeping accommodation	70	81	83	91
satisfied with atmosphere	33	58	50	59
wants to stay as long as possible	36	56	20	27
would prefer accommodation in digs	40	29	56	62
feels he is unlikely to become independent	43	64	57	47

equivalent period in the Camberwell Reception Centre in 1973 and in the St Mungo Community in 1976. They were younger and more likely to have been admitted to a psychiatric hospital and to have had a problem with alcohol. Men at the Camberwell Reception Centre and Cedars Lodge were more likely to have served a prison sentence than men in the other two settings. The Camberwell Reception Centre contained by far the highest proportion of men born in England and Wales.

As discussed earlier, one of the main aims of the research was to compare the attitudes of men in smaller reception centres with equivalent groups (in terms of length of stay) at the Camberwell Reception Centre and the St Mungo Community. Very few men, in any of the organizations, said that they had ever been asked for suggestions by staff. Men at St Mungo's and Cedars Lodge were more likely to say that this had occurred. On most other indices the attitudes of men in the smaller centres were closer to those of St Mungo's than of Camberwell residents. In particular, over 80 per cent of men at St Mungo's, Pound Lodge, and Cedars Lodge said that staff were friendly. Men at Pound Lodge and Cedars Lodge were much more likely than men at Camberwell to say that they talked to staff often. Similarly, there was little difference between the St Mungo Community and the two smaller centres in the men's attitudes to other residents. The men in the smaller centres were much more likely to identify their situation with that of other destitute men than were Camberwell residents. When asked about amenities the men at the smaller centres were, on the whole, rather more satisfied than the St Mungo residents. Men at Cedars Lodge, for example, were more likely to be satisfied with their food and sleeping accommodation than St Mungo residents, and just as likely to find the atmosphere of their accommodation pleasant. On all these indices the attitudes of Camberwell men were much less favourable. The Camberwell men were more likely than the other three groups to feel confident about their ability to lead an independent life. When asked how long they wanted to remain in residence the responses of men in the two smaller centres were closer to the Camberwell than to the St Mungo group. Between a fifth and quarter wanted to remain in the centres as long as they could. This compared with a third (36 per cent) of the Camberwell men and over half (56 per cent) of St Mungo residents. Men in Pound Lodge and Cedars Lodge were more likely, upon discharge, to want to acquire their own accommodation (such

Table 6(4):   *Follow-up status, at two, four, and six months after discharge, of 'case-paper' men at Pound Lodge and Cedars Lodge*

status	Pound Lodge (N102)			Cedars Lodge (N108)		
	2 mths	4 mths	6 mths	2 mths	4 mths	6 mths
still resident	0	0	0	4	4	4
readmitted	11	9	5	0	3	1
own accommodation	13	13	12	10	10	10
with relatives	8	7	6	4	5	5
other reception centres	8	6	4	26	24	23
lodging houses	5	3	3	1	1	2
hospital	2	1	0	3	1	1
prison	1	1	1	5	2	1
other	2	3	2	13	11	9
untraced	52	60	69	42	47	52
% of total group in own accommodation or with relatives	20.5	19.6	17.6	12.9	13.8	13.8

as a flat), rather than live in a hostel or with a landlady. Their attitudes were closer to Camberwell than St Mungo's in this respect.

In order to assess the resettlement outcome of men contacting the centres efforts were made to establish their whereabouts after discharge. To this end the research team attempted to trace four groups of men (the two case-paper and the two interviewed groups) two, four, and six months after discharge. The results of the enquiry are given in *Tables 6(4)* and *6(5)*.

Most of the men who could be traced were not living in their own accommodation.* The men most likely to move to independent accommodation (13 per cent at the two month follow-up) were the Pound Lodge case-paper group. These men seemed, on the basis of the enquiries at four and six months, to have maintained this settlement. It is likely that fewer of these men, compared with the Cedars

---

*The demographic and social characteristics of the traced and untraced groups were similar so that one can tentatively assume there were no substantial differences in outcome.

Table 6(5):   *Follow-up status, at two, four, and six months after discharge, of interviewed men at Pound Lodge and Cedars Lodge*

status	Pound Lodge (N30)			Cedars Lodge (N34)		
	2 mths	4 mths	6 mths	2 mths	4 mths	6 mths
still resident	6	6	6	4	4	4
readmitted	4	6	1	6	6	3
own accommodation	0	0	0	3	2	2
with relatives	1	1	1	0	0	0
other reception centres	3	4	2	9	8	7
lodging houses	2	1	1	3	2	2
hospital	0	0	0	0	0	1
prison	0	0	0	0	0	0
other	1	1	1	2	3	2
untraced	13	11	18	7	9	13
% of total group in own accommodation or with relatives	2.9	2.9	2.9	8.8	5.8	5.8

Lodge clientele, had experienced prolonged destitution so that presumably their resettlement posed fewer difficulties. Some men, too, had gone to live with relatives. Again this was more likely among the Pound Lodge case-paper group (8 per cent at the two month follow-up).

About half of the traced men in the case-paper groups and over three-quarters of the equivalent interviewed men were in contact with reception centres, lodging houses, and voluntary organizations working with destitute men. A similar pattern was apparent after the follow-up (during a comparable period) of residents in the St Mungo Community (see Chapter 4). Compared with Pound Lodge men the Cedars Lodge groups were more likely to make use of reception centres. This probably reflects the differences in the characteristics of these groups described on page 135. The Cedars Lodge men were more often handicapped and perhaps less able than the Pound Lodge group to compete successfully for other forms of accommodation. It may, however, be that Cedars Lodge men, having received special consideration, were more willing to make further use of reception centres.

Three hypotheses

A full discussion of these results, in the light of the material presented earlier in the book, will be deferred until the next chapter. Here, we shall consider the three hypotheses put forward before beginning the work at the two smaller centres and discuss whether such crude comparisons can offer a solid basis for drawing conclusions.

The first hypothesis was that there would be little difference between men using the different kinds of service for periods longer than three months. The fact that Camberwell men who previously would have moved 'into residence' were now transferred to Cedars Lodge makes this conclusion tautological and the similarity between Camberwell 'residents' and longer-stay men at St Mungo's had been observed earlier. The interesting fact is that Pound Lodge men who stayed for three months or more had very much the same characteristics as longer-stay men at Cedars Lodge, at Camberwell in 1973 and at St Mungo's. These are the more solitary, middle-aged to elderly, disabled clients, many of whom originally came from Scotland or Ireland. If anything, the men accumulating at the new reception centres are more handicapped than those at Camberwell in 1973 or St Mungo's in 1976. It is possible that pressure on a diminishing supply of lodging houses and cheap rooms, caused by high unemployment and the more frequent use of such accommodation by the unemployed 'able-bodied', is forcing the handicapped to have increasing recourse to reception centres as the only viable alternative to sleeping rough.

The second hypothesis was that the attitudes expressed by men at the smaller centres towards staff and amenities would be much the same as those of men at St Mungo's. The results confirmed this. The smaller centres seemed to facilitate frequent interaction and good relationships between residents and staff and satisfaction on this count was matched by satisfaction with amenities. On all the indices listed (food, sleeping accommodation, and atmosphere) men at the smaller centres in 1977 were much more satisfied than men at Camberwell had been in 1973 and, in most cases, they were also more satisfied than men at St Mungo's in 1976. A suggestion that reception centre staff, in general, are censorious and impersonal and thus foster alienation in clients is not supported by these results. It seems more likely that the buildings and amenities at Camberwell unfavourably influenced the attitudes of men and, to a lesser extent, of the staff.

The third hypothesis was that the outcome after discharge would reflect the disabilities of the men rather than any differences that might be found between the environment or regime of the organizations. Since we thought that these disabilities were likely to be much the same in the groups that stayed for three months or more (our first hypothesis, which was confirmed), it follows that the outcome would also be much the same. This was the case. Both smaller reception centre managers commented on the enormous problems involved in resettling their handicapped residents. They felt unable, on humanitarian grounds, to put pressure on the men to leave but saw little prospect of resettling them. The ready availability of psychiatric hospital beds and hostel places was crucial in this respect. One centre had a good relationship with its local hospital, the staff of which were sympathetic to the residents' needs and concerned to help them in any way that they could. At the other centre, however, hospital help left much to be desired. The local consultant was reluctant to admit men of no fixed abode, believing them to be unamenable to treatment, and consented to admission only in cases of crisis. The strain experienced by the centre's staff as a result of this was considerable. Hostel places were very few and hostel staff were reluctant to admit men who were severely handicapped. (For a similar situation, see Hewett, Ryan and Wing 1975). All the hostels demanded that prospective residents should either be working or should rapidly find a job. Thus, one centre manager described ex-residents who had, when placed in hostels, 'overstayed their welcome' since, although regularly paying rent, they had not found work. The great majority of hostel places were in unsupervised lodging houses and it was fairly common for residents receiving medication to relapse when referred to such accommodation.

The design and method of these studies had to be tailored to circumstances and were by no means ideal. The men and the staff at the various agencies were not closely comparable. The measures of attitude were crude and might have been affected by the settings in which the interviews were conducted. Many men were untraced at follow-up (though it is unlikely that substantial numbers of these had found settled accommodation). Moreover, St Mungo's is by no means characteristic of all voluntary organizations, nor are London reception centres characteristic of those in other parts of the country. Readers will be able to judge for themselves from the data presented how far our conclusions are justified. We think they are and that they have far-reaching implications which will be discussed in Chapter 7.

The 'peripatetic' survey

All the surveys so far considered, apart from that by Archard (1975), dealt with the problems of men who were in contact with some kind of helping agency, rather than with the problems of men 'on the streets'. This is because such people are widely dispersed, are mobile (either through choice or because they are frequently 'moved on'), and have little incentive to cooperate in a survey. The survey of 'skid row' by Edwards and his colleagues (1966), focused on men who accepted hand-outs at an East End soup kitchen. The St Mungo soup run provided similar opportunities. It was very difficult, however, to make an adequate assessment of the needs of men who drifted away in the dark after receiving their soup, in order to find a place to sleep, or to move elsewhere, or to avoid company.

During 1974–5, the research sociologist (JL) and Irene Barker, a St Mungo worker with several years experience of street work, systematically visited, at set times on the Wednesday of each week, six West End sites (such as the Embankment gardens) at which destitute men tended to pass their time. They had informal conversations with men who were willing to respond but did not attempt to ask for names or make any kind of standard enquiry. No attempt was made to disguise the fact that they were interested to know about the circumstances of the men at these sites. They came to know many of the 'regulars' very well and were often able to pick up information about men they did not talk to directly.

During the year, 393 different men were seen at six sites but 116 of them only appeared on one or a few occasions and the observers did not get to know anything about them. These men were not recognised as having used the St Mungo services. There was sufficient information about the other 277 (only thirty-three of whom had not been in the Marmite shelter or in a St Mungo house) to make a very rough classification of predominant problems into five sub-groups, as follows:

members of drinking schools	58	(21%)
heavy drinkers not belonging to schools	72	(26%)
'dossers' without a drink problem	108	(39%)
casual workers	28	(10%)
'tramps'	11	(4%)

Because of the large proportion of men whose characteristics were not known* and because of the fact that men seen at these six West End sites might not have been typical of destitute men in general, no general conclusions can be drawn. The figures are given simply because they are the best available for men actually observed on the streets.

The largest sub-group consisted of 'dossers' (the name the men themselves used when referring to each other), who were chronically unemployed and moved between lodging houses, shelters, reception centres, and sleeping rough, but did not have a serious drink problem. Nearly all of them had used the St Mungo night shelter and some had been admitted to houses for short periods. It was not possible to say what the main causes of their destitution were although many were known to have been in psychiatric hospitals or were evidently physically disabled. This sub-group overlapped with the next largest, composed of men with a severe drink problem, who were part of the same accommodation circuit but whose lives were conditioned by a need for alcohol. Nearly all of them had used the Marmite Shelter. They tended to be solitary individuals who joined others only when it was necessary to pool resources for a bottle or to cadge a cigarette. Some had been in St Mungo houses but had never stayed long. The rapid turnover of these men during the early stages of the action research, when the houses were 'dry', has already been described.

Members of drinking schools made up the third largest sub-group. Archard (1975) has given an account of their existence. They use shelters on occasions and know where the best handouts can be obtained but are rarely prepared to accept offers of longer-term accommodation. Apart from the Simon Community's 'crude spirit shelter' and the 'wet' area of Marmite few attempts have been made in London to provide for the needs of those who cannot do without alcohol for the night. Most of the men in this sub-group observed during the 'peripatetic' survey were Scots or Irish. One fifth of them had not used St Mungo services, the rest had attended the night shelter (where there was a 'wet' area). None had settled in a St Mungo house for any length of time.

In the fourth sub-group there were twenty-eight men who had

---

* Many of these men probably fell into the category described by Tidmarsh and Wood (1972a) as 'situational', i.e. they had temporary problems which entailed some disadvantage but were not part of the scene of long-term destitution. Others must have been 'dossers' on a wider circuit than those who stayed in London.

fairly regular though casual employment and usually lived in cheap rooms and lodging houses. All but one had used St Mungo houses or night shelter but only during periods of temporary embarrassment when funds were low or more favoured accommodation already booked up.

Only a tiny proportion (4 per cent) of the men observed could be designated as 'tramps', using this term in its old-fashioned, somewhat romantic, connotation. These few individuals did claim that they had voluntarily rejected worldly possessions and a settled existence. Such men are discriminating in their use of shelters and handouts and rarely stay long in one place.

At first sight, it is unsurprising that most of the 'known' men had been in contact with St Mungo services since, between them, the two observers had a close acquaintance with men who used the soup run, the night shelter and the houses. However, the 'unknown' men seen during the survey only appeared on one or a few occasions, and most were unknown also to the 'regulars', so that they were probably only temporarily destitute (if at all) or were 'passing through'. In that case, the large majority of men (277 or 70 per cent) who were 'known', only thirty-three of whom had not been in contact with St Mungo's, may be representative of the larger number of destitute men who sleep fairly regularly in central London.

It seems likely that day facilities of various kinds would have been used by many of these men had they been available. There was no equivalent, during the daytime, to the range of accommodation that could be selected from at night.

Day shelters, occupation centres, and workshops would probably attract regular users in the same way that night shelters do and could thus provide a valuable extra means of contact and extend the range of choice whereby men who wish to do so can occupy themselves. The only other alternative seems to be to wander the streets, occasionally standing alone or in small groups hoping not to be 'moved on'.

Summary

In spite of the differences in age, education, ideology, experience, and likely future career, the attitudes expressed by staff at St Mungo's and at the Camberwell Reception Centre were not greatly different. Camberwell staff, however, described a lower group (as opposed to individual) morale and were aware of the low esteem in which their work might be held by the general public. They were more likely to support a system of compulsory in-house tasks as a means of occupying residents and helping them help themselves. Both groups said, in general, that destitute men were disabled and disadvantaged rather than lazy and that insufficient facilities were available to help them. Residents who had stayed for three months or more in the two settings were more likely than new entrants to be middle-aged, solitary, disadvantaged, and disabled. The longer-stay men at Camberwell were less satisfied with amenities and gave less favourable opinions of staff than longer-stay men at St Mungo's.

At the smaller Battersea Annexe attitudes of staff and men were intermediate compared with the other two settings. Awareness of 'socially desirable' answers was possibly a factor explaining the discrepancy in attitudes expressed by Camberwell staff compared with those of Camberwell residents but the influence of the setting probably also played a large part. We thought that Camberwell staff would welcome an opportunity to work in a centre with more adequate facilities and that they would then be regarded as more supportive and friendly by residents.

This hypothesis was confirmed by a study of the attitudes of residents to staff at two smaller reception centres where buildings were more adequate; these were as favourable as those of men in St Mungo houses. The outcome, two months after discharge, of men leaving St Mungo's and the two smaller centres after a stay of three months or more, was much the same and gave rise to little suggestion that there was a likelihood that such men could return to live in their own accommodation or with relatives. Disability seemed the major determinant of outcome.

In a study of men who passed time during the day at various locations in the West End of London, it was discovered that two-thirds had used St Mungo services, particularly the night shelter. On the whole, this was a 'local' group, with very few vagrant members. More than half had an alcohol problem, divided approximately equally between members of drinking schools, who were very difficult to help because of their special socialization patterns, and more solitary drinkers. Another two-fifths were men 'on the circuit' between various kinds of accommodation, including lodging houses, who did not have an alcohol problem. Most had used St Mungo facilities but had not stayed for long. Many of these men would probably have used day facilities had they been available.

7 How best to help destitute men?

The common background of destitution

Beatrice Webb pointed out that preventing poverty was immeasurably more humane, more practical, and more economic than trying to relieve it. That was true in her day and some part of what she wanted has been achieved. We have principally been concerned, in this book, with the problems of men who live in extreme poverty; men who commonly sleep rough or make use of night shelters and reception centres. Some, at least, of those problems certainly can be relieved. However, before discussing various ways in which men already severely and chronically destitute can be helped, it is important to discuss whether our research, and that of earlier workers, provides any suggestions about prevention. This means widening the frame of reference to include men who, while not destitute to the same degree, are at high risk of becoming so. The users of common lodging houses form one such group, particularly since the supply of cheap accommodation began to dwindle in the early 1960s. Peter Wingfield Digby (1976) found that a quarter of the residents of hostels and lodging houses said they had used reception centres (but only 3 per cent had done so frequently) and 54 per cent had slept rough (14 per cent frequently, although this experience was usually quite recent). Long-term residents in sheltered institutions for the ill and disabled, or in prisons, form another vulnerable group because the philosophy of 'community care' has been easier to apply in the negative sense of discharging people from what is regarded as a harmful environment than in the positive sense of setting up new and more appropriate alternatives. Beyond these obviously vulnerable groups there are others in earlier and more hypothetical stages along the various paths that lead eventually to destitution.

Two types of problem stand out as being particularly common among the severely destitute. The first is the obvious one of social disadvantage, but this is not just a current problem; it has very often been evident since childhood. The men interviewed by Wood and Tidmarsh (1972a) at Camberwell Reception Centre had often come from large families in financial and housing difficulties. They did not do as well as average, intellectually or socially, at school; found themselves as teenagers in a market where few unskilled jobs were available and where accommodation for single people was scarce and expensive; circulated through a variety of living-in or institutional (e.g. armed forces) or casual employments, and built up no firm or lasting basis of savings, property, or social or family relationships. Very often, this process left the individual stranded in middle-age in run-down urban areas, and dependent on welfare benefits during long periods of unemployment. The temptations of alcohol, and the risk of imprisonment for minor offences, are added complications.

Since so many severely destitute men have passed through this prolonged 'apprenticeship' it is reasonable to suggest that any means of breaking the chain of events (and the earlier action were taken the better) would also prevent the eventual outcome. Providing subsid-ised accommodation for single people, job creation schemes (particu-larly for the unskilled), methods of income maintenance (OECD 1976), casework with vulnerable families (or families containing vulnerable members), are ideas that have been canvassed, although their efficacy has not been fully demonstrated.

A report on Young Scotsmen in London (West End Coordinated Voluntary Service 1976) describing a recent increase in the numbers of young people from Strathclyde who come south to look for work but find, not only that they must remain unemployed but that the price of decent accommodation is entirely beyond their means, shows that the

long process described by Wood and Tidmarsh may now be tele-
scoped into a much shorter period. There seems to be little doubt that,
as unemployment rises and becomes more chronic in the most
deprived areas, more and more young people are affected, and it is not
only the most marginal youngsters who are at risk.

Since the time of the Minority Report of the Poor Law Commission
it has been generally accepted that much poverty can be prevented.
We should recognize the progress that has been made during the past
half century and ensure that it continues, in the belief that the
numbers of the severely destitute will also be reduced thereby.
Although this issue lies beyond the scope of our own research we have
little doubt that a case can be made for further primary preventive
action.

This kind of action will not, however, be enough. Earlier social
disadvantage is not *the* cause of severe destitution. Most people living
in deprived areas, and most members even of severely disadvantaged
and vulnerable families, do not become severely destitute. The second
factor that is obviously contributory is disability. Our own studies
amply confirm the results of previous workers. Physical illnesses and
disabilities though common, are as frequently a result as a cause of
destitution, though the history of Mr Frost, on page 95, illustrates
their importance. The severe brain damage suffered by Mr Davies
and Mr King (see pages 94 and 98) clearly contributed to their
becoming destitute as did the severe schizophrenic impairments of
Mr Jenkins (page 98). Very few of the men who accumulated in St
Mungo houses towards the end of the period of research, or in the
residential sections of Camberwell or the smaller reception centres,
had single disabilities. Mr Ingram (page 97) illustrates the multiplicity of disabilities that can occur together.

The majority of people who develop such severely disabling conditions do not end up in reception centres. Disability is no more *the*
cause of severe destitution than is social disadvantage. Nevertheless,
the rundown of the large mental hospitals, and the inadequate
provision made after discharge, are substantial contributory factors
and present obvious targets for preventive action.

It has been suggested that the studies of destitute men which
demonstrated the frequency of various kinds of disability has 'led
research away from sociological aspects' (Donnison 1975). We cannot see any justification for this statement or for the common accompanying argument that a description of personal disabilities and

difficulties is no more than a process of stereotyped 'labelling' (Beresford 1976). Identifying the diversity of an individual's problems (which are never purely social or purely biological) and considering the epidemiological (i.e. the group) aspects of disability, are part of the long tradition of social medicine which has played a substantial part in the development of the preventive as well as the relieving policies of the 'welfare state'. This tradition will continue to enrich social research and we have no doubt that most social scientists will continue to welcome it. Whatever the reason for the lack of good social research in the past it will not be put right by searching for scapegoats.

If neither disability nor social disadvantage is sufficient, in itself, to cause destitution, the combination is often deadly. The two factors can be independent of each other but there is frequently an interaction between them. Alcoholism may cause both disability and disadvantage. Florid schizophrenia may be preceded by a history of social impairment stretching back into childhood so that the first acute attack supervenes in someone who is already socially isolated. Prolonged disability and prolonged disadvantage (and even more the combination of the two) frequently lead to depression, lowered self-esteem, and lack of confidence, which are in themselves disabling.

Many of those who have set up or worked in services for destitute people have posited a third type of factor. Anton Wallich-Clifford thought that social inadequacy,

'. . .the inability to face up to demands, responsibilities, and pressures of life within the normal framework of society, is as handicapping to the individual as physical disablement and mental illness. Social inadequacy causes overcrowded prisons, overloaded psychiatric wards, and overfull dosshouses. The misfit is the casualty, not the casual, of our affluent society.'

We do not think that this concept of 'inadequacy' has much explanatory value; it is simply a one-word summary of a long history of social disablement for which there is no obvious cause. However, in this descriptive sense it does give a name to a problem. There are people who become destitute although others with apparently more severe disabilities or disadvantages do not. Terms like 'personality disorder' carry the same connotation.

There are, however, some less obvious factors at work. Some disabled individuals do not become severely destitute purely because a sheltered or institutional environment is available and they are content to accept it. In other cases, it is because they have an exceptional determination to keep going with as little external help as possible. Equally, some severely destitute people preserve their independence in their own way, even at the expense of giving up what most people regard as essential comforts, while others simply wish to avoid all responsibility and as much social interaction as possible. The element of choice is often (and rightly) played down but the negative value attached to a term like 'inadequacy' can obscure qualities which, in other circumstances, would be found admirable. We have not found it necessary to use such terms in this book and do not think that anything essential has been lost thereby.

Whatever may be thought of the merits of further state intervention to prevent social disadvantage, or of the much more obvious benefits to be obtained from improving the health and social services for chronically disabled people, there is no doubt that severe destitution will remain a serious and urgent problem for many years to come. This problem has been our main concern and in the remainder of this chapter we shall draw upon the results of our own and earlier research in order to suggest what might be done to help destitute men more effectively.

The last days of the Camberwell Reception Centre?

The first suggestion about closing the Camberwell Reception Centre was made in 1939 but action was put off 'temporarily' because of the war. Since then its disadvantages have always been evident to successive authorities but large numbers of men (8,000 in 1972 according to Tidmarsh and Wood) continued to use it. A substantial number of the places were occupied by men 'in residence', most of them disabled in various ways, who could not easily be moved elsewhere. It was rarely possible to identify a health area or local authority that would accept responsibility for providing care or housing for such people.

As with the large mental hospitals which are also theoretically being 'phased out', the recognition that closure must eventually come, together with the difficulty of providing decent alternatives, has actually made matters worse during the interim. In part, at least, the hiatus has been due to over-optimism in the post-war period that preventive measures would drastically reduce the numbers of disadvantaged and disabled people at risk of becoming severely destitute.

A comparison in 1973 of the attitudes of staff at Camberwell with those of St Mungo workers showed that the former were well aware of their public image. Individual members of staff did not differ very much in what they said about destitute men or about their own sense of job satisfaction, but Camberwell staff rated the general morale at the Centre as low and public attitudes towards their work as critical and rejecting. The residents themselves differentiated more sharply between the two settings. Residents who had stayed at Camberwell for more than three months hardly ever said they were asked for suggestions by staff, only a fifth said they often talked to staff, and less than a half said that staff seemed friendly. In all these respects, men who had stayed more than three months in St Mungo houses gave much more favourable answers. Overall satisfaction with the 'social atmosphere' in the two settings was also markedly different (33 per cent compared with 70 per cent).

These differences might suggest that individual staff members at Camberwell, when interviewed by the research team, responded in the knowledge that certain attitudes would be regarded as socially desirable. Before placing this interpretation on the results it is worthwhile considering the situation at the Battersea annexe. This was a hostel set up principally for older long-term residents from Camberwell. The research team interviewed only those under sixty-five but 85 per cent of the sample were over fifty. Their experience of destitution and use of hospitals and prisons was much the same as for men at Camberwell. Their attitudes were intermediate between those of residents at Camberwell and in St Mungo houses. In particular, they gave a much more favourable account of their contacts with staff and of their satisfaction with amenities than residents at Camberwell. Staff responses at Battersea were also intermediate but closer to those of St Mungo workers than to Camberwell staff.

Thus, although a 'social desirability factor' possibly did affect the replies of staff at Camberwell and, to a lesser extent, at Battersea, it seemed likely that staff (and residents' opinions of them) were also affected by their surroundings. It seemed reasonable to suggest that Camberwell staff, working in more encouraging conditions, would be better able to be friendly and supportive and would attract more favourable comments from residents. Although they were very different people from the young St Mungo workers, we thought that, potentially, they could make quite as important a contribution.

Given the size, the grim workhouse buildings, the lack of amenities, and the feeling of scepticism that Camberwell would ever be closed, together with the recognition by staff of a low group morale and rejecting public attitudes, it is perhaps surprising that allegations of neglect and ill-treatment have been uncommon. The results of several commissions of enquiry into analogous situations in other large institutions suggest that small groups of staff can behave inhumanely in such conditions and that other staff and management can turn a blind eye. No-one who has read the records of 'single care' of the mentally ill in the early part of the nineteenth century, when sufferers were kept chained by themselves in cellars or garrets by hired keepers, can believe that size or officialdom alone is the cause of such cruelty. We cannot, of course, comment on recent allegations of brutality at Camberwell but, since the allegations have been made public, we would emphasize our own belief that the large majority of staff there would not only be able but would welcome the opportunity to make a more sizeable contribution to helping destitute men, given better working conditions.

The smaller reception centres

Unfortunately, the Battersea annexe was sited in buildings as old and unsatisfactory as those of Camberwell and had to be evacuated after a roof fell in. However, several smaller centres have been opened and others are planned so that closing Camberwell in the mid-1980s remains a possibility. Two of the smaller centres in London, Pound Lodge and Cedars Lodge, provided a useful opportunity for the research team to test ideas arising out of work at Camberwell, Battersea, and St Mungo's.

Although Cedars Lodge admits only men selected after a stay at Camberwell, while Pound Lodge accepts men 'from the streets', the longer-stay men at Pound Lodge have much the same background of disadvantage and disability as those at Cedars Lodge or Camberwell, which in turn are much the same as those of men who eventually accumulated in St Mungo houses. If anything, longer-term residents at the two smaller centres were even more likely to have slept rough for a year or more, to have been in psychiatric hospitals, and to have had a problem with alcohol than men at Camberwell or St Mungo's.

In accordance with our experience at Battersea, residents and staff at Pound Lodge and Cedars Lodge expressed (in 1977) largely favourable attitudes to each other and to the amenities. There was no difference from the results of the latest survey (a year earlier) of residents and workers in St Mungo houses. To this extent, therefore, the policy of replacing Camberwell by several smaller centres has been successful. There is still a question, however, of whether other alternatives would be just as viable and provide a higher quality of life. We shall return to this matter later.

So far as follow-up results are concerned there was very little difference between the various settings. The most complete follow-up was of thirty-four men discharged after at least three months' stay at Cedars Lodge, the whereabouts of twenty-seven of whom were known two months later. These men had been specially selected from Camberwell but only three had found their own accommodation; none was living with relatives and three were in lodging houses. A two-month follow-up is not long but it is probable that any improvement in skills or attitudes (including self-confidence) that occurs while at the centre (or in a St Mungo house) dissipates rapidly after discharge if better accommodation is not found (Wing 1966). Longer follow-up enquiries were made at St Mungo's without any suggestion of better results being achieved later on. Our hypothesis that disability rather than type of regime determined subsequent outcome seemed justified.

It should not be forgotten that a substantial proportion of the work at many reception centres is of a quite different kind. Of the eighty-five beds at Pound Lodge, thirty-six are for 'casual' admissions and there is a high turnover. Tidmarsh and Wood found that more than a quarter of the 8,000 people admitted to Camberwell in 1972 were migrant workers, people temporarily unemployed, or men with other 'situational' problems. The centres offer a few nights' lodging, vocational guidance, and help in sorting out welfare problems. Most of these men are not severely or chronically destitute. Another quarter of the men admitted have a serious alcohol problem. Yet another quarter are handicapped, some of whom can be referred to more appropriate agencies. The enormous variety of problems is evident.

An alternative system?

We drew attention in Chapter 1 to the disillusion created among those who worked with destitute people when the high expectations fostered during the postwar period proved illusory. Among the alternative philosophies put forward, that of the Simon Community was particularly influential. The young workers of one of its offshoots, the St Mungo Community, founded in May 1969, believed, as Simon workers had done, that it was necessary to close the gap between themselves and the men they were trying to help by sharing the same living conditions in the houses they set up. The idea of 'Community' was a powerful one. Contact with the men was made on the regular nightly soup run. Men who wished to do so could return to an assessment centre, move to a house, and then on to less sheltered settings. If they wished, they could become 'workers'. This compelling vision, powered by a variety of philosophies (from religious to political), provided the motive force during the early years of St Mungo's and intermittently thereafter. The idealism, dedication, and sheer hard work in uncomfortable conditions of the men and women who gave up à year or two of their lives to work in the Community without expectation of material reward was heartwarming and the settings they created in the houses were as different from that of Camberwell Reception Centre as can be imagined.

Nevertheless, from the time, in September 1971, when the research team began to observe events, until late in 1975, it could not be said that the men who entered the houses were either resettled (in the sense of finding better accommodation outside the Community) or that they even stayed long enough, in most cases, to be much affected by the milieu of the houses. The recommendations made by the research team during this period, most of which were acted upon, made no difference. In retrospect, it seems likely that a major reason for this was the fact that men met on the soup run who were offered, and who accepted, a place in houses were those who found it relatively easy to talk to soup run workers and could appreciate the value of a few nights' shelter. Few of them, however, were interested in a longer stay. (About 15 per cent of the men admitted used to stay for more than three months.) Those who were solitary and avoided contact with others were less likely to be noticed by workers, less likely to form a relationship, and less likely to be offered or to accept a place in one of the houses. There was also, at least initially, a bias against accepting men with psychiatric disabilities.

It was not until the night shelter had been open for long enough to make it obvious that a considerable group of 'regulars' was building up, that the routine assessment system allowed the selection of men who would not have been sufficiently forthcoming to be picked out on the soup run. Having used the night shelter for some time the transition to one of the houses did not involve a substantial increase in responsibility, and the men began to settle down. In this way, St Mungo houses filled with disabled people. Paradoxically, however, they were not men who could take an active part in community life; nearly all the effort of communication was made by the workers.

A few of the men did go on to bed-sitters but there were not sufficient of these to allow much movement through the houses. By 1976, therefore, St Mungo's faced precisely the same problem as the reception centres, that of accumulation. A wide range of services had been set up by this time. Apart from the soup run and the three groups of houses, the night shelter served something of the function of a reception centre for casual attenders, and there was a block of bedsitters (Lennox Buildings) and some lodging house accommodation in the former Charing Cross Hospital.

This chain of services begins closer to the streets than do the operations of the reception centres and it extends well beyond the reception centres in its variety of care and accommodation. But it is still not enough. There is little interaction with other services although, when collaboration did occur (as with the community psychiatric nurse who visited one group of houses) it was much appreciated by workers and valuable to residents. Contact with the social services was particularly poor. But no voluntary organization can be self-sufficient. It can fill some of the gaps, draw attention to others, and campaign for better services all round, but it cannot replace the statutory system, it has no power to require the health and social services to carry out their responsibilities properly, nor can it deal with problems of early prevention.

Moreover, the growth in size of St Mungo's brought with it some of the disadvantages of an increasing bureaucracy. There had, of course, been conflicts from the beginning, just as there had in the Simon Community, but the conflicts themselves became, in the end, bureaucratized, with some of the workers joining a trade union in order to resist management pressures they thought unacceptable. Workers were also more experienced and better paid and many group leaders had professional qualifications.

Thus, as the reception centre system painfully, and by fits and starts, became less formal and authoritarian and looked forward to a time when Camberwell really would be closed, an alternative voluntary organization was becoming more institutional. The houses and bedsitters constituted only a small part of its activities and one that had become completely static. Management concentrated most attention on units such as the night shelter and Charing Cross which, while they catered for much larger numbers, simply provided extra accommodation of low quality. Like the Supplementary Benefits Commission, they did not regard housing and caring for the disabled as their primary duty. The motivation and ideals of the young volunteer workers which had powered the progress of the Community in the early days were no longer a distinctive feature of the whole organization.

Other voluntary organizations provide services which help to fill in gaps. The Salvation Army has a longer tradition of service than any. It provides a quarter of all the beds available for homeless single people and has bail hostels, detoxification units, and rehabilitation centres for alcoholism. Numerous small charities provide useful help for destitute people and preserve a vital independence from the statutory system.

The provisions of the Housing (Homeless Persons) Act, 1977 and of the Housing Corporation circulars 1/77 (which announced that hostel projects run by registered housing associations providing a degree of support might be eligible for a Housing Corporation grant) and 4/78 (which is a guide to housing associations on the development and management of housing for single people) have not yet been sufficiently exploited by voluntary agencies. Bodies such as CHAR (1973a, b; 1974) (Campaign for Single Homeless People) undertake an essential function in coordination and in keeping the problems of homeless single people in the public eye and we hope they will become more influential.

We conclude, therefore, that there can be no *alternative* system; only complements and supplements to statutory services.

Concepts of rehabilitation and resettlement

Two preliminary steps must be taken before we can attempt a definition of 'rehabilitation'. The first consists of a statement of aims concerning the group of people needing help, or of individual members of the group. This will be determined by the values of those running the helping organization, taking into account, as far as they can, the values of those they are trying to help and what resources they have available. The second step consists of an assessment of the problems which handicap the achievement of these aims; in the case of destitute men, as we have seen, disadvantage and disability, together with adverse personal reactions such as a loss of self-esteem and self-confidence. Rehabilitation can then be defined in terms of the methods used to overcome the handicaps in order to achieve the aims. Clearly, the underlying philosophy of the helping organization (which may not always be the one presented publicly) will determine the aims, the problems that are investigated, and therefore the techniques used.

The Supplementary Benefits Commission has a duty to 'make provision whereby persons without a settled way of living may be influenced to lead a more settled life'. Resettlement includes not only enabling people to live independently in the community but referring those who need longer-term or more specialized care to the appropriate agency. The Simon Community looked for Christ 'in even the most abandoned character' and tried to provide a permissive small group setting in which men could re-learn how to make social relationships. The Salvation Army is guided by 'its dominant interest in the spiritual welfare of people. Salvationists believe that regeneration is more important than rehabilitation' (Salvation Army 1976).

We did not find that several months' experience in one of the smaller reception centres or in one of the St Mungo houses had any obvious effect on outcome. The kind of help that newly homeless men are given, which together with temporary shelter often proves quite effective, is not, of course, suitable for the chronically disabled and disadvantaged. The philosophy of the organization does not very much affect the outcome if this is measured in purely practical terms; its value probably lies much more in motivating staff.

The central fact about the men who accumulate in the residential sections of reception centres and in the longer-term houses of organizations like St Mungo's is that they are disabled, often with multiple disabilities. This may not be the sole reason why they become destitute but, together with a lack of social support, and complicated by a secondary loss of self-esteem and self-confidence, it is the main reason why they remain so. The experience of the action research at St Mungo's is of interest to those who would like to help such men. When they were met on the soup run, initially, many were passively or actively withdrawn and workers did not see them as participating members of a 'community'. Once they were given the chance of attending a night shelter, where very minimal demands were made on them, a proportion began to attend regularly, of their own accord, not being put off even by having to attend a social security office to obtain money to pay for a ticket. Those who attended the shelter regularly were then more willing to accept an offer to try one of the houses. The 'participation' philosophy of the houses had not survived several years of experiment and men were not put under pressure to interact or take more responsibility than they found comfortable. We believe that this was why so many did in fact stay. A few, however, were able to accept greater responsibility and move to bed-sitters which were visited regularly by non-residential workers but were otherwise independent.

This model consisted of a chain of options, each one realistic in the sense that it did not require a substantial advance to make use of it and in the sense that a move forward was not a leap into the unknown. Each step involved the offer of a choice, and a decision by the man concerned. Both elements were required. The chain led from the soup run to a bed-sitter but each step was quite small. Moreover, those who found they could go so far but no further were able to stay at a given level, without rejection, and without undue pressure to move forward again. In this model, rehabilitation is seen as an 'enabling' rather than a 'changing' process, although change may very well occur. Progress is always seen as positive, even when it does not lead to full 'resettlement'.

This particular chain was concerned with accommodation and, as we have seen, there were limitations at the level of houses and even more at the level of bedsitters, which restricted the amount of movement possible. Nevertheless, the idea is a good one. It recalls Donal Early's two 'ladders' of rehabilitation, one domestic and one vocational (Early 1965). It has to be accepted that some men will not wish to step even on to the lowest rung. Others, like the members of drinking schools described by Peter Archard, will construct their own social environment and only accept such help as enables them to maintain it. Until men have been offered real choices and have been able to determine, by trial and error, how far they are able to go, and until adequate provision is made at each level for those who cannot move further, it cannot be said that a service for destitute men is adequate.

The quality of accommodation provided in the night shelter is poor, justifiable only by contrast with sleeping rough. This comparison is the right one to make (since a more sizeable gap would be difficult to bridge), but only if plenty of opportunity is provided to move to better housing. This is true at all levels. The St Mungo houses are more comfortable than the night shelter, and provide a more natural environment than 100-bed reception centres, but there are insufficient funds to provide more of them. The bed-sitters that allow more normal accommodation are even scarcer.

From the early days of the Simon Community, there has been a recognition that small houses, with a non-authoritarian but caring atmosphere, should be more attractive and provide a higher quality of life than any of the alternatives – sleeping rough, 'pads', shelters, reception centres, large hostels, and so on. Studies of small hostels for alcoholics (e.g. by Tim Cook 1975) and by Shirley Otto and Jim Orford (1978)) gave substance to this ideal. The large-scale survey by Digby (1976) showed that half of the men in common lodging houses said they would prefer accommodation in small houses or flats. Nevertheless, few of these studies have shown that men actually do settle in such accommodation, in the sense that they stay long enough to regard it as a 'home'.

This is not true of hostels and group homes for handicapped people. A series of studies of the accommodation for people who have been in psychiatric hospitals have shown that the opposite type of problem has occurred (Clark and Cooper 1960; Hewett, Ryan, and Wing 1975; Wing and Hailey 1972; Wing and Olsen 1979). People have not 'moved on', even when the ideal of the unit was that they should be 'rehabilitated' and so become independent. Voluntary and local authority hostels for the mentally disabled have provided a good quality of life and a homelike atmosphere and the main complaint of doctors and nurses is that there is a pitiful lack of such accommodation.

The St Mungo houses illustrate this latter point. They cannot be regarded as 'high quality' in the sense of the hotel attributes that comfortable people would regard as important. In fact, seen through comfortable eyes, they are distinctly grubby and shabby. That does not particularly seem to worry men who have spent much time sleeping out and who have progressed to a house from a night shelter. By the same token, however, some men undoubtedly could have appreciated higher standards and would have been able to settle very well in the local authority hostels and group homes studied by Hewett and Ryan (Hewett 1979; Hewett, Ryan, and Wing 1975; Ryan 1979; Ryan and Wing 1979). Some of the most severely handicapped people would have felt at home in the hospital-hostel described by Acker, Wykes, and Wing (1979). Unfortunately, housing and care of this quality is not sufficiently available even for people who have a 'parish'.

The vocational 'ladder' is even more sparsely provided for. Ideally, there should be day as well as night shelters, occupation centres, training units, and sheltered workshops for those who can benefit from them, and provision for gradually moving into the stream of services provided by the Department of Employment. Reception centres are better able to make such contacts than voluntary organizations but the chain of options is seriously incomplete. An experimental day centre for homeless single people has recently been reported but little experience has yet been gathered (Social Work Service Group 1978).

We think that the 'enabling' model of rehabilitation is the right one for chronically destitute men. However, it does raise difficult problems of provision: first, the necessity of providing a chain of housing and vocational opportunities at closely spaced levels, so that there are no unbridgeable gaps to deter a man who is able to move forward; second, the necessity to provide for an accumulation of men, at each level, who are unable to progress further. This second problem – that of accumulation – has bedevilled all services for handicapped people and, in the case of the destitute, it raises a special difficulty which also has a long and sad history, that of the 'parish of origin'.

A third dimension of need cuts across the need for housing and for occupational facilities. This is the need for care, treatment, and support. The section in Chapter 4, on two St Mungo houses, illustrates the kind of care given by the house workers to severely disabled residents, including two with marked memory impairment, several with schizophrenia, and many with multiple problems. Help from general practitioners, community psychiatric nurses, and social workers was invaluable when it could be found but the general picture was one of a scarcity of such provision for chronically destitute men.

In our view, the institution of closer links between resettlement agencies and local medical and social services should accompany increases in the provision of contact and residential facilities for destitute men, as should a considerable expansion in back-up support (for example, visiting social service and nursing consultants) provided at each stage of the resettlement process. Because of the wide variety of physical and psychiatric disabilities exhibited by destitute men specialist help is a necessary complement to 'contact' and the provision of accommodation. Thus, the 1973 DHSS Circular 'Community Services for Alcoholics' concluded that hostel staff '. . . should ideally have access to medical, psychiatric, psychological and social work support and work closely with the staff of the treatment units in their area. It would be advisable for these local social services departments and probation and aftercare committees to appoint liaison officers to each hostel so that they can support staff and advise on 'general policy and selection of residents' (DHSS 1973). The Department hoped, with the assistance of selected authorities, to provide some areas with a comprehensive system of preventive, treatment, and rehabilitative services. Such 'centres of excellence' were to serve as a model for other localities.

At present, however, such provision exists only on paper. Despite surveys and reports ('Habitual Drunken Offenders' (Home Office 1971) is a notable example) which have 'diagnosed' the needs of destitute groups, and despite a large measure of agreement concerning the kinds of provision that are required (see, for example, the reports and circulars cited above) very little has been done. The situation of the St Mungo houses illustrates this well enough. The quality of help the houses received from statutory services was poor. The community nurse who visited one group of houses was much appreciated, as was the link with the psychiatric hospital and its out-patient clinic. Very little help, however, was available from the local Social Services Departments. The general practitioner services also left much to be desired. Specialized forms of domestic and vocational training were not available either at day centres or in workshops.

In part, this lack of provision (and marked lack of action to remedy the deficiency) probably reflects, as Archard has suggested, the persisting implicit distinction between the deserving and undeserving poor.

Contact services

Making contact with destitute men is a necessary preliminary to trying to help them. The ordinary services provided by health and local authorities are often unwelcoming or even rejecting. Hospital casualty departments, for example, or social work intake teams, find it difficult to treat a destitute man on his merits; local authority housing departments even more so.

Contact services form the first stage in the process of resettlement and should be provided in all areas known to be frequented by destitute men. They provide immediate physical and psychological help for the men contacting them and act as a link between their clients and the medical and social services. These roles, involving a close interaction with individuals who may be reluctant to engage in any interpersonal communication, involve considerable patience and tact. Their essence has been summarized by Titmuss (1970: 15).

'Listening not to oneself but to what others may be trying to say is an essential part of social diagnosis as well as medical diagnosis. From it flows "sympathetic consciousness". It also has a value in itself, social, cultural and moral, in implying and expressing respect for the dignity of others in a world which values speed, busyness, efficiency and activity.'

By listening without imposing conditions, and by the avoidance of comments which could be interpreted as censorious, contact staff are often able to establish relationships and so assess attitudes and needs. The extent to which the men will respond to offers of help will, of course, vary between individuals, although the experience of the St Mungo night shelter suggests that a relatively informal, regular contact can succeed in assisting large numbers of men to take advantage of a wider range of services. Some practical comments concerning the day-to-day running of contact services, derived from experience of the St Mungo night shelter, are presented elsewhere (Leach 1979).

The provision of contact services has received some government support during the last decade, particular emphasis being placed on the need to reach homeless alcoholics. Thus, the Report of the Home Office Working Party on 'Habitual Drunken Offenders' recommended the experimental provision of a 'shop front' in one of the main Skid Row areas of London. The most important feature of this service was to be its accessibility to men on the streets. The nature of the premises (given that their location was sound) was not, in the Working Party's view, of particular importance.

'What is vital however is that the centre is known to the vagrant alcoholic population of the area as a place in which there is an ever

open door to immediate help *for their drinking problem* . . . its success
as a motivational or pre-treatment agency is more likely to depend
on its accessibility; its constant availability (a twenty-four-hour
service, for example, is desirable); the absence of an 'institutional'
atmosphere; and the approach and attitudes of the staff' (Home
Office 1971: 120).

This venture had some success in that men did make use of its services
and remained in contact with them. Cook, presenting data concerning the first two years of operation of shop fronts run by the Alcoholics
Recovery Project, found that about one third of the men coming to
these establishments were self-referred. Of a sample of 100 men, 47
per cent were still in touch by letter, telephone or personal visit,
twelve months after contact (Cook 1975).

The role of contact services in referring men to residential accommodation was shown in Chapter 4, which discussed the activities of
the St Mungo soup run and night shelter. In addition to this function,
however, these services facilitate the provision of other kinds of help.
Of particular importance, given the morbidity of destitute men and
the exigencies of living rough, is their role of liaison with local medical
services. In some cases, medical treatment is provided by the contact
agency itself. A Manchester night shelter, for example, was visited
regularly by a mobile surgery, manned voluntarily by two local GPs.
Over 300 people were treated during a six-month period. Following
this venture arrangements were made to register shelter residents as
temporary patients at a local Health Centre. Occasional visits to the
shelter were made by doctors treating those too sick to attend the
regular surgery. At the time this activity was reported efforts were
being made to establish a surgery at the shelter itself.

Contact facilities tend, by nature, to be makeshift and unsophisti-
cated. Their primary aim is to be situated 'in the heart of districts,
indeed in the very streets, where the largest concentrations of potential clients are to be found' (Home Office 1971: 120). Given this aim,
and the fact that the nature of the premises is not, in itself, important
(provided that minimum standards of comfort are stipulated and
enforced) the potential to expand this provision, without a prohibitive
increase in resources, is considerable. The inner cities, where destitute
men tend to congregate, contain many premises which could be
utilized as contact centres. St Mungo's adaptation of the derelict
Marmite factory in Vauxhall provides an example. Simon Commun-

ity volunteers, similarly, took over a disused rag storage workhouse in the East End of London, opposite a bomb site inhabited by a large school of meths drinkers, and invited the latter to move in. The men who slept on mattresses on the ground floor were still drinking and were allowed to bring their bottles into the premises. To criticism of this policy the volunteers replied that their aim was 'to provide a home, companionship, and food for schools of drinkers. If thrown out the men would revert to sleeping rough and have even less chance of giving up meths' (Lapping 1967: 50). Their eventual aim was to provide a house to accommodate men who 'made a start' by staying dry in the shelter.

Who should take responsibility?

The problem of accumulation, to which we have made frequent reference, remains the predominant difficulty in providing for the chronically and severely destitute, and for homeless single people in general. It can no longer be met by setting up large institutions which attempt to undertake all the multiplicity of functions required. There is little point, however, in abolishing large institutions if no alternatives, of higher quality, are set up to replace them. The 'enabling' model of rehabilitation which we favour requires a wide variety of contact services, domestic and vocational 'ladders' with the possibility of sheltered vocational and residential provision at each level, and an adequate supply of subsidised housing (bedsitters, group homes, supervised lodgings, and small hotels) at the top.

The voluntary sector has a vital part to play which is complementary to the official system rather than alternative to it. Above all, the health and social services and local housing authorities, which at the moment grossly neglect their obligation to help *all* those in need, whether destitute or not, ought to begin to play their full part. This duty has been pointed out many times, however, without much effect. We hope that the public protests of bodies such as Campaign for Single Homeless People will gradually begin to make an impact. However, the old problem of the 'parish of origin' and the fact that many severely destitute people are not willing to accept the solutions provided by official organizations, pose substantial problems.

It is indeed unfair to expect the health and social authorities of vulnerable inner city areas to bear the brunt of providing for people who originate all over the country. The problem is national rather than local. Because of the common combination of disability with disadvantage the government department with greatest experience and expertise is the Department of Health and Social Security, although the Department of Employment, the Department of the Environment, and the Home Office share some of the responsibility. The designation of the severely destitute as part of the 'single homeless' can give rise to a rather facile assumption that the main solution is to provide adequate housing. This is certainly the case up to a point, particularly for people in common lodging houses, but the men we have chiefly been discussing present far more complex problems.

We do not think that encouragement given to voluntary bodies to make use of the opportunities to set up housing associations, and central grants to such organizations which complement the statutory services, will be sufficient. Central drive and coordination are necessary. We may take as example, that of the Housing (Homeless Persons) Act of 1977, which requires local authorities to take action 'whenever someone approaches them for help in relation to accommodation and the authority have reason to believe he or she may be homeless or threatened with homelessness'. Although homeless single people are not excluded, it is clear that the provisions of the Act are mainly concerned with homeless families and this is how local authorities have interpreted it. It is very unlikely that, without central funding, many severely destitute people (who rarely 'approach' authority anyway) would be helped in this way. Of men discharged from hospital or prison the Act specifies that 'it may be better for him to return to the area where he lived previously'. Similarly, the exploitation of the very complex opportunities summarized in Housing Corporation Circulars 2/78 and 4/78 could only be carried out on a small scale by voluntary bodies, whereas a coordinated national effort is required.

Another solution that has often been canvassed for London is that GLC boroughs should jointly take responsibility, but a Working Party report in 1977, while expressing cautious approval that something should one day be done, did not encourage hopes of decisive action in the near future. Since this represented three years work, it seems unlikely that much can be expected from this source. In any case, most destitute men living in London were not born or brought up there and ratepayers are not usually charitably inclined towards such causes. Certainly, it is ridiculous to expect Tower Hamlets, Southwark, and Camden to shoulder most of the burden.

The measures taken up till now are well intentioned and permit measurable progress to be made, but without central direction that progress will be extremely slow. In our view, the Department of Health and Social Security (as a whole, not simply the SBC) has a clear responsibility for taking the lead.

One of the first areas for action is to establish small hostels and group homes, and day facilities, in the neighbourhood of the smaller reception centres, using central funds to do so. This would enable reception centres to concentrate on the shorter-stay entrants and not to have to take on a spurious 'rehabilitation' function. Voluntary organizations should also be encouraged to expand their house and bedsitter accommodation so as to allow more movement from the streets. As voluntary organizations grow in size it becomes necessary to create a licensing system and inspectorate, because neglect and ill-treatment are not solely found in public institutions.

The next priority should be to devise means of requiring the health and social services to give single homeless people the same priority afforded to the rest of the community.* In the case of certain local authorities this will mean devising means of giving direct aid for setting up and staffing houses and day facilities. In the case of health areas it will mean encouraging the provision of hospital-hostels (since local authorities will not provide for the severely disabled), finding ways (perhaps through special payments) to encourage general practitioners and community nurses to give more time to domiciliary work in hostels and group homes, and ensuring that casualty departments in inner-city areas are able to cope with the difficult medical emergencies presented by destitute men.

The third priority is the most difficult: to monitor and coordinate the efforts made by government departments, by local authorities and health authorities in high risk areas, and by voluntary organizations. It may very well be true that, in the long run, local housing authorities should be responsible for providing and maintaining most buildings needed by people who would otherwise be destitute, with specialist

---

* We recognize that, in the case of severe disability, health and social services do not always provide a very effective service even for those who have family support. Some suggestions for remedying this lack have been made elsewhere and apply equally to destitute people (Wing and Olsen 1979).

help as necessary from public social and health services, and gaps filled by local voluntary organizations (which will also critically review the whole system). We do not see such plans maturing in the near future. Tidy administrative solutions are most unlikely to work; people simply will not fit into them. During the next ten to twenty years we need a flexible and multicentred system with strong support from central funds. That entails central direction.

Central direction in turn requires public support and this is where the wheel comes full circle. The Secretary of State for Social Services, introducing a White Paper on 'Better Services for the Mentally Ill' (DHSS 1975), argued that, 'we have to recognise that the pace at which community based care can be introduced depends not only on resources but on the pace of response of the community itself'. In the early days of the New Poor Law there was a similar tension. The principle of less eligibility simply could not be applied when 'legitimate' farm labourers were nearly starving. That tension led, in the end, to abandoning the New Poor Law altogether (Fraser 1976), or at least to trying to get away from it. But the destitute, the chronically mentally ill, the severely mentally retarded and severely demented old people, are still the least acceptable and least welcomed members of society. If they have their own social supports, well and good. If not, they are someone else's problem. Between these two extremes, human callousness and human kindness, democratic governments have to try to provide a realistic lead. Just as, in the 1830s, 'the most frequent battle between central and local administration was that between a reforming bureaucracy anxious to raise standards and parsimonious guardians bent on economy' (Fraser 1976), so now, only a central government department can provide both the motivation and the resources necessary to help the most severely disadvantaged. Public opinion, as represented in local government, places the 'single homeless' at the lowest level of priority. Public opinion, as represented by central government, can afford to act on higher principles.

Bibliography

ABEL-SMITH, B. AND TOWNSEND, P. (1965) *The Poor and the Poorest*. London: Bell.

ACKER, C., WYKES, T. AND WING, J. K. (1979) A Hospital-hostel for the 'New-long-stay'. MRC Social Psychiatry Unit: Unpublished.

ANSTRUTHER, I. (1973) *The Scandal of the Andover Workhouse*. London: Geoffrey Ble.

APTE, R. Z. (1968) *Halfway Houses*. London: Bell.

ARCHARD, P. (1973) Sad, Bad or Mad: Society's Confused response to the Skid Row Alcoholic. In R. Bailey and J. Young (eds), *Contemporary Social Problems in Britain*. Farnborough: D. C. Heath.

—— (1975) *The Bottle Won't Leave You. A Study of Homeless Alcoholics and their Guardians*. Alcoholics Recovery Project, 47 Addington Square, London SE5.

ATKINSON, A. B. (1969) *Poverty in Britain and the Reform of Social Security*. London: Cambridge University Press.

BECKER, H. S. (1963) *Outsiders. Studies in the Sociology of Deviance*. Glencoe: Free Press.

BERESFORD, P. (1976) Is this our problem? *New Psychiatry* 24 June: 12–15.

BERRY, C. AND ORWIN, A. (1966) No Fixed Abode. A Survey of Mental Hospital Admissions. *British Journal of Psychiatry* **112**: 1019–27.

BESWICK, J. A. (1978) *Caring for Dossers: Towards a Scientific Evaluation of the Work of Cardiff Cyrenians.* Unpublished report.

BLAU, P. M. (1964) *Exchange and Power in Social Life.* New York: Wiley.

BRANDON, D. (1972) Lodgings. *New Society:* 597–8.

—— (1974) *Homeless.* London: Sheldon Press.

—— (1975) Research in Progress. Report of the proceedings of a meeting held on 13 March 1975 to discuss research into the needs of homeless single people. p. 3. DHSS: Unpublished.

BROWN, M. (1969) *Introduction to Social Administration in Britain.* London: Hutchinson.

BROWN, M. AND WINYARD, S. (1975) *Low Pay in Hotels and Catering.* London: Low Pay Unit.

BROWN, M. J. (ed) (1974) *Social Issues and the Social Services.* London: Knight.

BUTTERWORTH, E. AND HOLMAN, R. (eds) (1975) *Social Welfare in Modern Britain.* London: Fontana.

CAMPAIGN FOR THE HOMELESS AND ROOTLESS (1973a) *Campaign Charter.* London: CHAR.

—— (1973b) *The Rights and Needs of Single Homeless People.* London: CHAR.

—— (1974) *Drunken Neglect: The Failure to Provide Alternatives to Prison for the Homeless Alcoholic.* London: CHAR.

CLARK, D. H. AND COOPER, L. W. (1960) Psychiatric Halfway Hostel: a Cambridge Experiment. *Lancet* **i**: 588–90.

COHEN, S. (1972) *Folk Devils and Moral Panics. The Creation of the Mods and Rockers.* London: MacGibbon and Kee.

COMMITTEE ON CHILD HEALTH SERVICES (1976) Report: *Fit for the Future.* Chairman: S. D. M. Court, Cmnd. 6684. London: HMSO.

COMMITTEE ON ONE-PARENT FAMILIES (1974) Report: Cmnd. 5629 and 5629-1. London: HMSO.

COMMUNITY RELATIONS COMMISSION (1974) *Unemployment and Homelessness.* London: HMSO.

COOK, T. (1975) *Vagrant Alcoholics.* London: Routledge and Kegan Paul.

CREER, C. AND WING, J. K. (1974) *Schizophrenia at Home.* London:

National Schizophrenia Fellowship, 79 Victoria Road, Surbiton, Surrey KT6 4NS.

CROSSLEY, B. AND DENMARK, J. C. (1969) Community Care – A Study of the Psychiatric Morbidity of a Salvation Army Hostel. *British Journal of Sociology*: 443–9.

Daily Telegraph (1977a) 31 October.

Daily Telegraph (1977b) 15 November.

DEPARTMENT OF EDUCATION AND SCIENCE (1967) *Children and their Primary Schools. A Report of the Central Advisory Council for Education (England)*. London: HMSO.

DEPARTMENT OF HEALTH AND SOCIAL SECURITY (1973) *Community Services for Alcoholics*. Circular 21/73. London: HMSO.

—— (1975) *Better Services for the Mentally Ill*. Cmnd. 6233. London: HMSO.

DIAMOND, G. M. (1972) *Alone with no Home*. Unpublished.

DIGBY, P. W. (1976) *Hostels and Lodgings for Single People*. London: HMSO.

DONNISON, D. (1971) No More Reports. *New Society* **17**: 921–2.

DONNISON, D. V. (1975) Introduction. *Report of the Proceedings of a Meeting held on 13 March 1975 to Discuss Research into the Needs of Homeless Single People*. London: DHSS. Unpublished.

DOUGLAS, J. W. B. (1968) *All our Futures: a Longitudinal Study of Secondary Education*. London: Peter Davies.

EARLY, D. (1965) Domestic Resettlement and Economic Rehabilitation. In H. Freeman (ed), *Psychiatric Hospital Care*. London: Balliere, Tindall, and Cassell.

EDWARDS, G., HAWKER, A., WILLIAMSON, V. AND HENSMAN, C. (1966) London's Skid Row. *Lancet* **i**: 249–52.

EDWARDS, G., WILLIAMSON, V., HAWKER, A., HENSMAN, C., AND POSTOYAN, S. (1968) Census of a Reception Centre. *British Journal of Psychiatry* **114**: 1031–9.

ETZIONI, A. (1970) Two Approaches to Organizational Analysis: A Critique and a Suggestion. In O. Grusky and G. A. Miller (eds) *The Sociology of Organizations*. Glencoe: Free Press.

FESTINGER, L. (1957) *A Theory of Cognitive Dissonance*. Row, Peterson, and Company.

FORDER, A. (1966) *Social Casework and Administration*. London: Faber and Faber.

FRASER, D. (1976) Introduction to: *The New Poor Law in the Nineteenth Century*. London: Macmillan.

GERARD, D. L. AND HOUSTON, L. G. (1953) Family Setting and the Social Ecology of Schizophrenia. *Psychiatric Quarterly* **27**: 90–101.

GOFFMAN, E. (1959) The Moral Career of the Mental Patient. *Psychiatry* **22**: 123–42.

—— (1961) On the Characteristics of Total Institutions. In D. R. Cressey (ed) *The Prison*. New York: Holt, Rinehart and Winston.

Halsbury's Laws of England (1959). Third edition. Vol. 27. London: Butterworth.

HALSEY, A. H. (1970) Social Scientists and Governments. *Times Literary Supplement*: 249–51.

—— (1973) *Educational Priority – EPA Policies and Problems*. London: HMSO.

HARE, E. H. (1956) Family Setting and the Urban Distribution of Schizophrenia. *Journal of Mental Science* **102**: 753–60.

HEWETT, S. (1979) Somewhere to Live. In R. Olsen (ed) *Alternative Patterns of Residential Care for Discharged Psychiatric Patients*. London: BASW.

HEWETT, S., RYAN, P., AND WING, J. K. (1975) Living Without the Mental Hospitals. *Journal of Social Policy* **4**: 391–404.

HOME OFFICE (1971) *Habitual Drunken Offenders. Report of the Working Party*. London: HMSO.

HUNT, D. (1973) Disablement. In I. Henderson (ed), *The New Poor*. London: Peter Owen.

HYMAN, H., WRIGHT, C. R., AND HOPKINS, T. K. (1962) *Applications of Methods of Evaluation*. Berkeley: University of California Press.

JONES, K. (1972) *A History of the Mental Health Service*. London: Routledge and Kegan Paul.

KANTER, R. M. (1972) *Commitment and Community, Communes and Utopias in Sociological Perspective*. Boston: Harvard University Press.

KATZ, A. H. (1964) *Parents of the Handicapped*. Springfield: Thomas.

LAIDLAW, S. A. (1956) *Glasgow Common Lodging-houses and the People Living in Them*. Glasgow Corporation, Health and Welfare Committee. Unpublished.

LAPPING, A. (1967) The Meths Drinkers Remain. *New Society* **10**: 50–1.

LEACH, J. (1979) Providing for the Destitute. In J. K. Wing and R. Olsen (eds), *Community Care for the Mentally Disabled*. London: Oxford University Press.

LEACH, J. AND WING, J. K. (1978) The Effectiveness of a Service for Helping Destitute Men. *British Journal of Psychiatry* **133**: 481–92.

LEES, R. AND SMITH, G. (1975) *Action Research in Community Development*. London: Routledge and Kegan Paul.

LIPSET, S. M. (1960) *Political Man. The Social Bases of Politics*. London: Heinemann.

LODGE PATCH, I. C. (1970) Homeless Men – a London Survey. *Proceedings of the Royal Society of Medicine* **63**: 437–41.

MACLEAN, M. AND JEFFERYS, M. (1974) Disability and Deprivation. In D. Wedderburn (ed) *Poverty, Inequality and Class Structure*. London: Cambridge University Press.

MANN, S. AND CREE, W. (1976) 'New' Long-stay Patients: A National Sample of 15 Mental Hospitals in England and Wales, 1972–3. *Psychological Medicine* **6**: 603–16.

MARRIS, P. AND REIN, M. (1967) *Dilemmas of Social Reform*. London: Routledge and Kegan Paul.

MARSDEN, D. (1969) *Mothers Alone*. Harmondsworth: Penguin Books.

MATTHEWS, G. (1968) Philosophy, Methods and Aims of the Simon Community. *Case Conference* **15**: 356–8.

MCCRORY, L. (1975) *Sick and Homeless in the Grassmarket*. Edinburgh: Social Work Department.

MERTON, R. K. (1968) *Social Theory and Social Structure*. Glencoe: Free Press.

MICHELS, R. (1966) *Political Parties*. Glencoe: Free Press.

MINISTRY OF HEALTH (1946) Public Assistance Circular 136/46.

NATIONAL ASSISTANCE BOARD (1966) *Homeless Single Persons*. London: HMSO.

NATIONAL ECONOMIC DEVELOPMENT OFFICE (1975) *Manpower Policy in the Hotels and Restaurant Industry*. London: NEDO.

NIGHTINGALE, B. (1973) *Charities*. London: Allen Lane.

OLLENDORF, R. J. V. AND MORGAN, A. (1968) Survey of Residents in the Camberwell Reception Centre. Report to the National Assistance Board. Unpublished.

ORGANIZATION FOR ECONOMIC CO-OPERATION AND DEVELOPMENT (1976) Public Expenditures on Income Maintenance.

OTTO, S. AND ORFORD, J. (1978) *Not Quite Like Home: Small Hostels for Alcoholics and Others*. Chichester: Wiley.

PAGE, P. (1964) Report to the National Assistance Board. Unpublished.

—— (1965) Camberwell Reception Centre. *New Society* **5**: 18–21.

PINKER, R. (1971) *Social Theory and Social Policy*. London: Heinemann.

PRIEST, R. G. (1971) The Edinburgh Homeless. *American Journal of Psychotherapy* **25**: 194–213.

PRITCHARD, G. (1969) Survey of Repeating Casual Population of Camberwell Reception Centre. Report to the Ministry of Social Security. Unpublished.

ROLLIN, H. (1963) Social and Legal Repercussions of the Mental Health Act. *British Medical Journal* **1**: 786–8.

ROONEY, R. AND WOOLF, R. (1975) *Claimant to be Doubted?* Edinburgh: Citizens Rights Office.

ROTHMAN, D. J. (1971) *The Discovery of the Asylum*. Boston: Little, Brown and Co.

RYAN, P. (1979) Residential Care for the Mentally Disabled. In J. K. Wing and R. Olsen (eds), *Community Care for the Mentally Disabled*. London: Oxford University Press.

RYAN, P. AND WING, J. K. (1979) Patterns of Residential Care. In R. Olsen (ed), *Alternative Patterns of Residential Care for Discharged Psychiatric Patients*. London: British Association of Social Workers.

SAINSBURY, E. (1977) *The Personal Social Services*. London: Pitman.

SALVATION ARMY (1976) *Annual Report*. London: Salvation Army.

SANDFORD, J. (1971) *Down and Out in Britain*. London: Peter Owen.

SARGAISON, E. M. (1954) *Growing Old in Common Lodgings*. London: Nuffield Provincial Hospitals Trust.

SCHEFF, T. J. (1966) *Being Mentally Ill*. Chicago: Aldine.

SCOTT, R., GASKELL, P. G. AND MORRELL, D. C. (1966) Patients Who Reside in Common Lodging Houses. *British Medical Journal* **2**: 1561–4.

SHEARER, A. (1977) Extra Costs. *New Society* **41**: 129–130.

SHILS, E. A. (1951) The Study of the Primary Group. In H. D. Laswell and D. Lerner (eds), *The Policy Sciences*. Palo Alto, California: Standford University Press.

SINFIELD, A. (1969) *Which Way for Social Work?* London: Fabian Society.

SKINNER, F. W. (1969) *Physical Disability and Community Care: A Study of the Prevalence and Nature of Disability in Relation to Environmental Characteristics and Social Services in a London Borough*. London: Bedford Square Press.

SOCIAL WORK SERVICE GROUP, DHSS (1978) Day Centres for Homeless Single People. *Social Work Service* **15**: 36–8.

STEWART, J. (1975) *Of No Fixed Abode: Vagrancy and the Welfare State*. Manchester: Manchester University Press.

SUPPLEMENTARY BENEFITS COMMISSION (1977) *Annual Report for 1976*. Chapter 5. London: HMSO.

TIDMARSH, D. AND WOOD, S. (1972a) *Report to DHSS on Research at Camberwell Reception Centre*. London: Institute of Psychiatry. Unpublished.

—— (1972b) Psychiatric Aspects of Destitution. In J. K. Wing and A. M. Hailey (eds), *Evaluating a Community Psychiatric Service*. London Oxford University Press.

TITMUSS, R. M. (1968) *Commitment to Welfare*. London: George Allen and Unwin.

TITMUSS, R. (1970) Introduction to *Helping the Aged*. by E. M. Goldberg. London: George Allen and Unwin.

TOWNSEND, P. (1957) *The Family Life of Old People*. London: Routledge and Kegan Paul.

—— (1962) *The Last Refuge*. London: Routledge and Kegan Paul.

—— (1975) *Sociology and Social Policy*. London: Allen Lane.

TULLY, J. B. (1970) My Friend 'Simon'; Some Realisations After Working for the London Simon Community. *Psyclops* **2**: Published by the Department of Psychology, North East London Polytechnic.

TURNER, J. (1978) One-parent Families: the Undeserving Poor? *New Society* **45**: 11–12.

WALLICH-CLIFFORD, A. (1968) *The Simon Scene*. London: Housman.

—— (1973) Quoted by: Henderson, I. Vagrancy. In I. Henderson (ed), *The New Poor*. London: Peter Owen.

—— (1974) *No Fixed Abode*. London: Macmillan.

WEBB, S. AND WEBB, B. (1909) *The Break-up of the Poor Law: Being Part One of the Minority Report of the Poor Law Commission*. London: Longmans, Green and Co.

—— (1929) *English Poor Law History. Part 2: The Last Hundred Years*. London: Longmans, Green and Co.

WEST END COORDINATED VOLUNTARY SERVICES (1976) *Young Scots in London*. Unpublished.

WHITELEY, J. S. (1958) Sociological Aspects of Schizophrenia. *Mental Hygiene* **42**: 497–503.

—— (1970) Proceedings of the Royal Society of Medicine. Report of a Meeting held on 11 November 1969: 446.

WING, J. K. (1966) Social and Psychological Changes in a Rehabilitation Unit. *Social Psychiatry* **1**: 21–8.

—— (1972) Principles of Evaluation. In J. K. Wing and A. M. Hailey (eds), *Evaluating a Community Psychiatric Service*. London: Oxford University Press.

—— (1978) *Reasoning about Madness*. London: Oxford University Press.

WING, J. K. AND BROWN, G. W. (1970) *Institutionalism and Schizophrenia*. London: Cambridge University Press.

WING, J. K. AND HAILEY, A. M. (1972) *Evaluating a Community Psychiatric Service*. London: Oxford University Press.

WING, J. K. AND OLSEN, R. (eds) (1979) *Social Care for the Mentally Disabled*. London: Oxford University Press.

WING, L., WING, J. K., GRIFFITH, D. AND STEVENS, B. (1972) An Epidemiological and Experimental Evaluation of Industrial Rehabilitation of Chronic Psychotic Patients in the Community. In J. K. Wing and A. M. Hailey (eds), *Evaluating a Community Psychiatric Service*. London: Oxford University Press.

WOOD, S. M. (1976) Camberwell Reception Centre: A Consideration of the Need for Health and Social Services of Homeless Single Men. *Journal of Social Policy* **5**: 389–99.

WOOD, S. M. (1979) The Social Conditions of Destitution. *Journal of Social Policy* **8**: 207–26.

Subject index

Name index